THE BRITISH JOURNAL OF PSYCHOLOGY

MONOGRAPH SUPPLEMENTS

XXVII

TESTS OF MUSICAL ABILITY
AND APPRECIATION

TESTS OF MUSICAL ABILITY
AND APPRECIATION

AN INVESTIGATION INTO THE
MEASUREMENT, DISTRIBUTION, AND DEVELOPMENT OF
MUSICAL CAPACITY

SECOND EDITION

BY

HERBERT WING

CAMBRIDGE
AT THE UNIVERSITY PRESS
1971

Published by the Syndics of the Cambridge University Press
Bentley House, 200 Euston Road, London NW1 2DB
American Branch: 32 East 57th Street, New York, N.Y. 10022
© Herbert Wing, 1968
Library of Congress Catalogue Card Number: 68-23919
ISBN 0 521 07251 4

First edition 1948
Second edition 1968
Reprinted 1970
Reprinted 1971

First printed in Great Britain at the University Press, Cambridge
Reprinted in Great Britain by Halstan & Co. Ltd. Amersham, Bucks.

PREFACE TO THE SECOND EDITION

Advantage is taken of this edition to include the music of the first three tests and some account of the revisions which the test has undergone.

My thanks are due to all those teachers of music who have kindly sent me suggestions for the improvement of the test from time to time. I am particularly grateful to the National Youth Orchestra and also to a group of New Zealand music teachers who were so good as to send me their results from taking the test while on a music course. Their comments and results were used in making the most recent revision of the test.

H.D.W.

Sheffield

1968

PREFACE TO THE FIRST EDITION

My thanks are due, above all, to Sir Cyril Burt who has encouraged and guided this work throughout its progress. His help has extended beyond the statistical and psychological side into the realm of music itself. The points in which he has helped me are too numerous to mention on every occasion in the text, but those who are familiar with his work will recognize his guiding hand in many portions of the investigation.

To Professor Hamley I am indebted for assistance on the educational aspects of the problem during the earlier stages of the work. I also owe a special debt of gratitude to Professor Flügel, Dr H. Lowery, the late Dr C. S. Myers, Professor T. H. Pear, Professor Rex Knight, Dr P. E. Vernon, and to many other psychologists and students of psychology who were good enough to submit themselves to the tests at a preliminary stage, and to offer constructive criticism.

Musicians, too, have been generous in giving their time and constructive criticism; they include the late Dr Geoffrey Shaw, Mr Cyril Winn, many teachers and performers and, especially, my wife.

I am also grateful to the London County Council and to those other educational authorities and educationists, who either have allowed me to test their pupils or students, or have assisted me in making such arrangements, often under trying conditions of evacuation and other pressing problems at school or college.

I have to acknowledge with gratitude the generosity of the University of London in contributing a grant from its Research Fund towards the expense of making the gramophone records, and of the British Psychological Society in contributing a grant towards the cost of publication of this Monograph.

Finally, my thanks are due to various members of the staff of Burderop Park Training College for their patient proof-reading.

H. D. W.

Burderop
1946

CONTENTS

CHAPTER I

THE GENERAL AIMS OF THE INVESTIGATION

The nature and assessment of musical ability and appreciation have been studied both from the pragmatic standpoint of those who are responsible for musical education, and from the scientific standpoint of psychologists who, though anxious to help in the solution of practical problems that arise in musical education, are primarily interested in theoretical issues. The musicians have worked for centuries by trial and error; the psychologists have for a comparatively short period conducted systematic experiments. Both have contributed to our present knowledge of the subject, but, at least as far as this country is concerned, they tend to disregard each other, although there are many common problems whose solution would probably be considerably hastened if the musician and the psychologist were each more sympathetic with, and cognizant of, the other's work and point of view.

In the present work an attempt has been made to satisfy both the musician and the psychologist by building on the result of a preliminary investigation with tests which had been drawn up from the musician's standpoint (165). It was thought that such tests might, if properly developed by psychological and associated statistical methods, form a means of assessing the musical capacity of individual subjects, especially those of school age. Moreover, their use might be extended to throw light on the mental processes involved not only in performing those tests, but also, since the tests were in themselves of a musical nature, on some aspects of listening to music in general. The distribution of musical capacity, the development of musical capacity with age, the general effect of home and school environment, were other problems it was hoped to attack. Further, it was desired to investigate the present, and other more efficient, modes of selecting children who would be suitable for training on a musical instrument, and to extend this investigation to the sphere of vocational guidance as an aid to those who might wish to follow music as a profession.

Since the standpoint of this investigation is nearer that of the musician than that of the physicist, the musical terms that are employed are to be understood in the sense in which they are ordinarily used by musicians, unless they are otherwise qualified. For example, 'listeners' are attentive hearers, and 'music' comprises styles acceptable to musicians and refers to played music. The word 'score', however, has a double meaning in a psychological work on music; it is here used in the usual psychological sense for the total marks obtained in a test, and 'notation' is used for all written music. The word 'musician' is used to include those who compose, conduct, perform, write about, or seriously listen to music.

The two terms which are central in this investigation are 'musical ability' and 'musical appreciation'. Many restrict the first term to the ability to play some musical instrument. But the teacher of music uses it in a wider sense that includes speed in learning to play, ability to perform the 'aural' tests discussed in the next chapter, and ability to carry out such musical activities as composing. Psychologists have also generally used the term in this extended sense, normally leaving out of account actual executive power,[1] and this procedure will be followed in the present investigation.

Musical appreciation, which is distinguished from musical ability both by musicians and by psychologists, is the power to recognize or evaluate artistic merit in music; it involves the deliberate aesthetic judgement of music as it actually exists in compositions rather than ability to solve problems connected with the elementary materials of which music is composed.

In music, as in other arts, the usual course in deciding what is good and what is bad is to take the opinion of the experts, and that is the course that has been followed here. The investigation of expert opinion tended to show not only that 'good' and 'bad' music can be clearly distinguished, but also that artistic merit can be assessed in the sense that reasonably similar pieces of music can be ranked.[2]

Musical appreciation and musical ability are obviously connected in some manner. Appreciation might logically be included as a form of musical ability, as it is an ability to distinguish the good from the bad, or less good, but it is preferred to keep the traditional meanings and to combine the two under the term 'musical capacity',[3] using 'ability' for the performance of certain problems with elementary

---

[1] Executive ability may be taken as one of the modes in which mental efficiency in dealing with musical material can manifest itself. It may be assumed that good performance upon an instrument demands mental musical efficiency as a pre-requisite, for a person's performance can hardly excel the limit set by his power to appreciate and therefore to criticize it. If those with high general mental efficiency in musical ability and appreciation are selected, the group will include all those who are likely to make good performers, although there will be some of them who lack factors of temperament, etc. which also play their part. Performance may therefore be taken as a subsidiary aspect of the mental capacity investigated in this work.

[2] An attempt was made to formulate the principles on which the judgement of the experts was based by giving them a list of twenty songs to rank, and asking for their introspections. The results obtained were in the nature of rather vague generalizations, but two characteristics generally agreed upon were that, in the first place, the musical composition should be properly integrated (Belaiew-Exemplarsky & Jaworsky (7) concluded that a melody can only be regarded as an aesthetic unity), and secondly, within this unity there should also exist an interesting diversity.

This is in agreement with an interesting proposition made by Burt (20) when he advances the idea that, at some future date, it might prove possible to arrive at a formula that would give an objective figure or index of the degree of beauty in any work of art, for the formula he has put forward as a first approximation involves these two points. He also takes into account the scope of apprehension of the listener (or viewer in the case of visual art) as this is an obvious limiting factor. It is as follows:

$$\text{Aesthetic Index (A.I.)} = \left(\exp \frac{D+I}{S}\right)^{-1},$$

where D is the number of items into which the work is differentiated;

    I is the number of relations integrating the items;

    S is the scope of apprehension under the usual conditions.

[3] It is not implied that this is of necessity a unitary capacity—it may be, and probably is, highly complex. A fuller description of the term can only be derived after it has been more extensively investigated by experimental procedure.

musical material, and 'appreciation' for discriminatory powers with music as actually performed.

Clearly both musical ability and musical appreciation are qualities of the whole mind; though they involve auditory discrimination they do not depend solely on the ear. Helmholtz (58) put forward the theory that 'the response of the ear is the key point of the psychology of music'. However, it seems more probable that the true view is the one put forward by Mursell (107) when he writes: 'Music depends essentially not on the stimuli which reach the external ear, nor on the response of the inner ear, but on the organizing and transforming operation of the mind.'

To a large extent this work rests on the assumption that there is a special mental capacity to deal with musical material, which, as was early proposed by Burt (17, 18) may, in part, be innate. If this be true (general musical opinion would support the assumption, and experimental evidence on the point will be advanced at a later stage) it is of practical as well as of theoretical interest to estimate it, and to trace its development, incidence, and so on.

Trials were made with such psychological tests as were available, but a conclusion was reached which was in agreement with Mursell's opinion that 'no satisfactory tests of musical aptitude as yet exist' (107). It therefore seemed necessary to compile a comprehensive series of new tests, to assess their relative merits, and, if a group factor underlying musical ability or appreciation or both existed, to select a short series of proved diagnostic value which could be standardized and used in this and in similar investigations.

CHAPTER II

TESTS AND EXAMINATIONS IN MUSICAL ABILITY AND APPRECIATION USED BY MUSICIANS

In psychological work which involves the drawing up of tests, it is usually taken for granted that a full preliminary investigation of the accepted practice among the professional workers in that trade or profession be first carried out. However, the published work of those psychologists who have compiled tests of musical capacity rarely, if ever, mention the existence or nature of the tests worked out by musicians themselves. These tests are well worthy of consideration, as they embody the results of experience over a very lengthy period, and are fertile in suggesting methods which, after suitable adaptation, might be used in psychological work.

For the most part the musicians' tests are designed either for the purpose of selection for scholarships and special coaching, or for qualifying tests before the award of a certificate or diploma. In common with tests in most other subjects they often involve considerable acquired knowledge, and, for this reason, sometimes fail, when used as scholarship tests, to select those who could best profit by the award. From the psychological point of view, although acquired knowledge is often a useful indication of interest and ability, any music test which is considerably affected by it is better avoided, owing to the very unequal opportunities which exist in musical instruction.

For scientific purposes the musicians' tests have other defects principally concerned with the musicians' tendency to use unstandardized methods. Thus, with the exception of examination papers in Harmony, Musical History, Form, etc., very few of the traditional tests are ever written out, but are applied according to the inspiration of the moment with all the variation in difficulty to which that procedure so commonly leads. As a result, in assessing a given child, the examiner will have only a rather vague (probably too high) estimate of the musical tasks which a child of that age should be able to perform, and he has no generally accepted method of expressing on some scale of marking the degree of retardation or advancement of the abnormal. Finally, although there is good agreement amongst the examiners on the value of a large number of the traditional tests, fads and fancies are not uncommon in musical examinations. Of course many of these criticisms might apply in large measure to examinations set in other subjects, but in music the position is worse because the training of the teacher has been largely an artistic one concerned with inspiration and impressions—almost the antithesis of statistical exactitude, whereas other teachers have inherited a tradition of written examinations and of keeping, and even scaling, marks. In the direction of the detection of the precocious, however, the music teacher is probably abreast of his colleagues because prognosis is a subject of as much interest to the music teacher as to the psychologist, for the child who is to train as a professional musician must specialize at a very early age.

Musicians themselves usually divide their examinations into three types: (a) aural tests, (b) paper work (written work), and (c) executive tests. In some examinations one or more of these sections may be omitted, e.g. for certain musical degrees there is no need to pass a test in actual playing. As the definition of musical capacity used for this investigation has, as is common in psychological work, been limited to mental efficiency, examinations in executive ability will only be discussed in so far as they involve mental abilities.

In aural examinations the examinee is set a musical problem on something which has been played; the problems usually involve questions on one or more of the following:

Intervals.
Chord analysis.
Cadences.
Discords.
Keys.
Musical dictation of time, melody or harmony.
Recognition of played music.
Reproduction of a short melody by singing or playing.

'Paper work' is a written examination on one or more of the following topics:
General musical knowledge including history of music, notation and form.
Recognizing well-known themes from the notation.
Writing suitable key changes.
Barring unbarred melodies.
Adding an answering phrase.
Harmonizing a melody.
The composition of chorale, song, fugue, or other work.

Viva voce examinations are occasionally set on similar material, and many of these tests have been adapted as exercises in extemporization for pianists. (153)

The more elementary written questions and most of the aural tests are problems concerning the elements of which music is composed and deal with what has been termed 'ability'. With the more advanced written tests and in executants' examinations, however, powers of appreciation (taste) may be tested to a very considerable extent. Thus the composition of a quartet, or even a song, will give abundant scope for taste, as will the playing of a piece by the executant. In the latter case the candidate is judged as much on the artistry of his performance as on his purely manipulative skill.

From the point of view of the psychologist concerned with the assessment of powers of appreciation, the procedure adopted at musical competitions or festivals is especially interesting. At such a competition we have an instance in ordinary musical procedure where the adjudicator has to estimate the merit of the performers on a scale of marks. The actual organization of a well-conducted musical competition is as close an approximation to a psychological test as it could be hoped to obtain in an aesthetic activity. Thus the conditions are made as standard as possible by careful classification of the candidates, using the same editions of music, often having the same accompanist for the different soloists, using the same assessment scale, and often having more than one judge—the hall and the judges are of course the same for all the candidates. The assessment forms may vary somewhat from competition to competition but the usual headings under which the judge has to enter marks are: Rhythm, Intensity Gradation (crescendos, etc.), Phrasing, Accuracy and General Impression. Accuracy will include that of pace, pitch and length of notes. The last vague heading is to allow for many unspecified factors such as ability to emphasize a part, e.g. to bring out an important melody, which often implies an appreciation of the form of the music, ability to play from memory, general attack, and so on.

It is interesting to note that where, as in the larger competitions, there may be a committee of judges, their opinions are usually in close agreement. This would indicate that there is something approaching unanimity among experts on the qualities that they think are desirable in music as performed, and secondly, that an executant's ability to give expression to these qualities may be graded with fair accuracy. If it is thus possible in musical practice, it should be feasible to adapt the procedure in order to evolve a corresponding psychological test. The method actually used in the present work to derive the first series of standardized tests in musical appreciation will be described later.

The judge falls short of the demands of the psychologist in that his marks tend to depart from any absolute scale, for his standard of marks may vary somewhat with the standard of the competition, e.g. he will probably be somewhat more lenient with his marking for the village festival than for the keenly contested professional competitions. The standard may also change to some extent as the general level of the competitors becomes apparent, or as the judge becomes fatigued with his task. In common with many other examinations, therefore, the marks of any individual have little meaning unless the standard of the judges and the competition be taken into account. However, the results show a sufficient degree of accuracy to encourage the hope that with a more standardized technique the process could be improved into a scientific method.

This brief survey shows that there are a variety of tests in use amongst musicians which they confidently expect will pick out those persons who have high musical capacity; further, that although the tests are not altogether fitted for psychological purposes, they suggest headings for the compilation of more suitable ones. Details of the individual tests and their psychological counterparts will be discussed in later chapters under the headings which have been mentioned and which, for convenience, are summarized below. In this list it has not been thought necessary as a rule to repeat a heading which comes under both an earlier and a later section in a very similar form, e.g. Cadences may form the subject of either aural or written questions, and an appreciation of the artistic use of Rhythm may be shown in either written or performed music. The tests numbered 1–11 are seen to be mainly of an ability (problem) type, while those numbered 12–20 are concerned mainly with appreciation (judgement).

(*a*) Aural Tests 1. Intervals.
       2. Chord Analysis.
       3. Cadences.
       4. Discord resolution.
       5. Key changes.
       6. Time Pattern Dictation.
       7. Dictation using tones:
         (i) Melodic Pattern Dictation.
         (ii) Harmonic Pattern Dictation.
       8. Recognizing Music.
       9. Memory.

(*b*) Paper Work 10. General Musical Knowledge.
       12. Rhythm.
       13. Melodic Shape.
       14. Harmony.
       15. Fitness.
       16. Creative Ability.

(*c*) Performance 17. Intensity.
       18. Phrasing.
       19. Pace (accuracy and variation).
       20. Emphasis of a Part–implying an appreciation of Form.
       11. Pitch Accuracy–for variable pitch instruments. (A test of ability rather than appreciation.)

CHAPTER III

THE ATOMISTIC TYPE OF PSYCHOLOGICAL MUSIC TEST

In psychological testing a style rather different from that used by musicians is required, for the aim in this case is to assess the capacity of any subject on a standardized scale of marks. Moreover, the examinees may be very young, or have received too little training to be able to demonstrate their musical capacity by the methods, often involving considerable knowledge, which are used by the music examiner. It was thought that a scientific series of psychological tests which could also be used by teachers and musicians should satisfy all, or most of, the following criteria:

1. Be acceptable in their basic principles to musicians.
2. Not be unduly influenced by training or opportunity.
3. Be comprehensive in their power to assess subjects of widely differing capacity.
4. Cover a sufficiently wide sample of musical talents.
5. Satisfy certain statistical criteria of reliability and intercorrelation.
6. Be suitable for repeated application to the same subjects without any great loss of efficiency.
7. Give a score which is easily evaluated on a standardized scale.
8. Be economical in the time required for their application.
9. Correlate well with an external criterion.
10. Be of practical use in musical education.
11. Be simple to apply.

The order given above is not one of their relative importance, but merely one which happens to be convenient for discussion in a later chapter where they will be dealt with in some detail.

The results of a survey of the psychological literature, in search of a series of tests which would satisfy these criteria, proved disappointing. It is, however, unnecessary to discuss the individual investigations in detail (this has already been done, to a large extent, in a previous work by the writer (165)), but some of the more important general criticisms to be levelled against them may be briefly mentioned:

(a) In compiling a series of tests workers have shown a tendency to ignore some of the qualities that the musician regards as desirable; in particular, the one common capacity that is demanded of all musicians, namely, appreciation, has been almost entirely neglected. In other cases investigators have relied on qualities which the musician regards as of little importance, e.g. absolute, or perfect, pitch.

(b) Many have taken only one aspect of music and have assumed that the results were diagnostic of general musical capacity.

(c) There is but scanty evidence that the tests have been developed beyond the stage in which they were used for the preliminary trials, e.g. by the use of a careful item analysis. The importance of this checking, item by item, of the test material will be made more apparent when the development of some of my own tests is considered.

(*d*) With many investigations such small groups have been used to test the validity of the assumptions made that the value or otherwise of the tests themselves is still open to considerable doubt.

(*e*) In very few cases have the test-scores been standardized; notable exceptions, however, are the batteries of Seashore and the similar one of Kwalwasser & Dykema.

(*f*) Some of the tests can only be applied to a narrow age range, or have the defect that they cannot be used again on the same subjects without a serious loss in efficiency. This renders them unsuitable for investigating the growth of musical capacity by re-testing children periodically.

(*g*) In very few cases has there been any attempt to find a validity coefficient by correlation with a teacher's ranking. In those few cases where it has been done the coefficient has been disappointingly low.

(*h*) Up to the present time the psychological tests of musical capacity have not, at least as far as this country is concerned, been adopted by the teachers of music. This may, in part, be due to conservatism, but as the music teacher is vitally interested in forecasting a child's possibility of success as an instrumental performer it is also a reflection on the efficiency of the tests in the eyes of the professional musician.

(*i*) The evaluation of the effect on the test scores of musical training and of opportunities to hear music seems to have been largely neglected.

These criticisms are not intended to apply to those investigations which have been concerned with such things as the threshold of intensity, or pitch, or smallest noticeable differences, or other similar work where the aim has not been to estimate general musical capacity; nor are they meant to apply to work that has been concerned with the investigation of reactions to music.

The psychological tests of musical capacity appear to fall into two sharply defined classes. On the one hand there are those that approximate to the tests used by the musician, and on the other there are those which have attempted to analyse music into its most elementary basic constituents and then to build up tests of a sensory type which aim at assessing these elementary constituents in their most exact form. As the latter attempt to go back to the simplest possible constituents of music they may be termed the 'atomistic' type of music tests. This style of testing is represented most fully by the Seashore tests, and these are practically the only series of standardized tests used by psychologists in this country.

Seashore's tests [133] are sufficiently well known not to need any very detailed description, but they may be briefly mentioned. The revised version, which has appeared comparatively recently, is not yet in use in England, and so the remarks which are made below refer to the original set of records. Although the new records are a somewhat closer approach to normal music, they are still of the same type, so that similar criticisms probably apply. The tests are as follows.

Original Version.

1. *Pitch.* Two pure tones are sounded consecutively; the subject is asked to state whether the second is higher or lower than the first. The difference may be as small as 1/200 of a tone.

2. *Time.* Three clicks are given; the subject is asked to state whether the interval of time between the second and third is longer or shorter than between the first and second.

3. *Intensity.* Two buzzer noises are sounded; the subject is asked to state whether the second is louder or softer than the first.

4. *Consonance.* Two intervals are sounded, and the subject is asked which pair blend better.

5. *Memory.* A number of consecutive notes, purposely selected to form no melodic line, are sounded; then follows a second playing which has one different note. The subject is asked to give the number of the altered note.

6. *Rhythm.* Two tapped time patterns are given, and the subject is asked to state whether they are the same or different.

Seashore's Revised Tests (137).

1. *Pitch.* As before. A pure tone of frequency 500 is used as the reference note.

2. *Time.* Filled time now replaces empty time.

3. *Intensity.* As before, but graded in decibel steps.

4. *Consonance.* Has been discarded and replaced by a test on *timbre* in which F sharp is played with six partials; the energy of the third is reduced and added to the fourth in steps of 10, 8·5, 7, 5·5, and 4 decibels. The subject is asked to choose the best timbre, i.e. that with the fourth in the smallest intensity.

5. *Memory.* As before, except that whole tones have replaced the previous semitone step.

6. *Rhythm.* Tones are now used instead of taps.

There are now three sets of records instead of one: (*a*) for an unselected group, (*b*) for musical groups, (*c*) for individual testing.

It is seen that the main change in the revised version is the removal of the test for one basic element (consonance) and the substitution of another (timbre).

Seashore's tests well merit the attention they have received, for they were pioneer work, and the first to be fully standardized. Moreover, it was essential that the atomistic approach to testing should be tried out, even though, as events have turned out, the experimental evidence concerning their weakness to predict musical ability has proved to be considerable. Criticisms have been levelled against them by Wright (171), Ogden (114), Mursell (106, 107), Heinlein (54), Highsmith (62), Brown (13), Brennan (11), Vernon (158) and also, indirectly, by Chadwick (27) and Farnsworth (39), who showed that the tests were hardly more efficient for predicting success than was a general intelligence test. Also, Larson (85) concluded that some of the Seashore tests were of little value in prediction. Others who have objected to the atomistic approach to the measurement of musical talent are Révész (123), More (102) and Lowery (90). Details of these psychological investigations are not included here as they have previously been described by the writer elsewhere (165).

Lowery, who is himself a musician, has also voiced objections to the tests from the musician's point of view (91). This is a matter which is not unimportant even to the psychologist, because the aim of the tests is to estimate musical capacity. If the musician or the potential musician can find little to interest him in the tests he is unlikely to do well, for, as is well known, it is necessary to secure the co-operation of those tested if a reliable estimate is to be obtained. There can be no doubt that in choosing pitch, tone, intensity, rhythm, harmony and memory, Seashore has taken some of the commonly accepted basic qualities which, when applied to tone, are of great interest to those of high musical capacity. However, he tests for them in such an elementary form that he leaves the realm of music, which is one of patterns and relationships in tone, and enters that of mere sensory perception—a matter outside the interest of the normal musician. It is almost parallel to testing for an appreciation of poetry by sensory ability to detect minute differences in letter structure. It is worth considering the individual tests from the point of view of their correspondence with the tasks actually required in performing or in listening to music, when this divorce from actual music is more clearly seen.

In the first (pitch) the examinee's limen for least noticeable difference in pitch is measured up to a limit of 1/200 of a tone. However, it is doubtful whether this degree of discrimination is ever required for actual playing, for Seashore's own very fine work on the performance of famous violinists has shown that even they tend to play to a Pythagorean scale, i.e. several vibrations away from the accompaniment. If the process of playing accurately in pitch were one of adjusting the instrument exactly to the accompaniment probably the Seashore test would prove more efficient. However, the process would appear to be one of getting true relationships between a given note and the notes which immediately precede and follow it, and bearing in mind, at the same time, the notes of the scale of the key in which one happens to be playing—a more complicated and more dynamic process than the Seashore test would appear to be assessing. To the musician, then, the Seashore test of pitch is too simple and measures too fine a degree of discrimination.

Tests 2 and 3 (time and intensity) are among the least satisfactory in the battery. This is probably because they are the two which are the most remote from actual music; this is not only because they deal with mere noise and not tones, which are after all the basis of all music, but also because they do not test for time and intensity as these are used in music. Thus, in performance, the correct length of a note does not appear to be based on a comparison with the note just played but on the dynamic rhythmic progression of the melody—especially in relation to movement towards a good climax. The correct use of intensity also is not merely a process of noticing that one note is louder than another, but of getting an intensity change that is suited to the melodic line and the whole character of the piece.

With regard to Test 4 (Consonance), which was based on somewhat out-of-date theories of harmony, detailed criticisms need not be given, as Seashore himself has found the test unsatisfactory and replaced it in favour of one on timbre. It is possible that the new test may suffer from some of the disadvantages of the old one, for timbre, like consonance, is a matter of personal choice.

Tests 5 and 6 (memory and rhythm) were found to be the best of the Seashore tests. This is probably because they are closer to actual music than any of the other tests. It was thought that the memory test would have been improved had it been made closer still by the use of tones with some kind of melodic line, for it is questionable whether a test for memory on nonsense material is fully valid for (musical) sense material. Reasons for this opinion are given later, together with a description of the adaptation of the Seashore test which I used.

Some of my personal experiences in using the Seashore tests with a group of 70 boys, aged 15–16 years, are probably of sufficient interest to be worth quoting in support of the above statements.

In this group the boy who was top in pitch (his Seashore percentile rank was actually 100) could not sing the simplest song in tune, although the quality of his voice was quite good. He apparently had little notion of the interval leaps that were required, for he would make a minor sixth where a fifth was needed and would change key without intention. He had had lessons on the violin for a considerable period but had given up in despair as he could not learn to play in tune.

A second boy in this group happened to be a very good violinist. He was sufficiently good to win a musical scholarship and to play violin concertos at concerts and he is now a professional player, yet his percentile rankings were only: Pitch 50, Intensity 51, Time 51, Consonance 78, Memory 83, and Rhythm 69. It is noteworthy that his highest scores are in those tests which have the most apparent connection with music; it may be that the low results in the others were simply due to the fact that the tests did not tap his musical interests, but the fact remains that had this group test been one where it was hoped to pick out those of high talent for special coaching, then this gifted boy would undoubtedly have remained undetected. The general results for this boy were considerably below that of another of the same age who, although he had had much the same tuition on the violin, was a very poor performer.

One of the boys was almost bottom in the Seashore pitch test with a percentile rank of only 15, although he could say at once how many notes were included in complicated chords played on the piano; in only 5 % of these trials did he ever make a mistake. He was a good pianist and a musical one as judged by the musicians' standards. Yet another boy who had a very low rank—actually of 18 in the time test—contradicted this in his performance, as he was a good solo singer who appeared to have no trouble with 'time' in music.

I did not know all these boys sufficiently well to be able to calculate a validity coefficient, but from the examples quoted it is obvious that it would not have been very high. Calculations by other investigators, based on music teachers' rankings, are discussed later and are seen to be very low and sometimes even negative. It would therefore appear that at the present stage in music testing it is not possible to name *a priori* isolated factors which, when added together, make up general musical capacity, and which can be tested for in isolation from music as normally heard. It would therefore seem preferable to approach the problem from an empirical view-point by finding out those tests which prove the most efficient as judged by their agreement with the music teacher's estimates. This is the method I have adopted.

CHAPTER IV

PSYCHOLOGICAL TESTS OF MUSICAL ABILITY WHICH USE MUSICAL MATERIAL

Other psychologists in the field of music—especially workers in this country—have preferred to use musical material in the composition of their tests, and their attitude, which is also my own, has been fairly expressed by Lowery (90), as follows: 'If it is required to test for the presence of innate musical tendencies, the entire isolation of constituent factors in music is not likely to be of great service; rather ought a factor which is considered sufficiently worthy of special attention to be brought into prominence with a musical background, the conditions of the testing being therefore analogous to those occurring in musical performance.' Mursell, too, states (107) that 'only the observations of the subject in various musical situations are a guide to the degree to which talent is present'.[1]

After a survey of such tests of a musical nature as could be found in psychological literature it was decided to use fresh material, because many of the accounts did not give the material used, and, where they did, it was felt that the music could be considerably improved. Furthermore, as the available evidence in literature was not sufficient to enable me to determine which were the best diagnostic types of test without actually employing them, I decided to compile a comprehensive list of the different types of test, and to compose a suitable version of each for group testing and then to select, by empirical methods, those best suited to the present purposes. The tests are discussed below. The order in which they will be taken will be the same as that already given for the musicians' tests, which will now be given in detail, together with their psychological counterparts and with my own group tests. In the following account the musical and psychological classifications cannot always exactly correspond, and tests concerned with attainments, or reaction to music, as well as the less original sub-tests of some investigators, have had to be omitted owing to lack of space. The account will, nevertheless, serve to indicate the main workers in the field. The tests are considered in two groups: first, in this chapter, the 'ability' tests, which deal with problems on elementary musical material, and in the next chapter, the 'appreciation' tests:

1. *Intervals*. Music is an art concerned with the relations between tones; of these relations obviously one of the most important is that of the pitch interval between various pairs of notes. It may reasonably be supposed that ability to detect the relation between two notes only might be indicative of the power to deal with the more complicated groups that occur in music as performed.

In musical examinations it is a common question in 'aural' work to strike an interval on the piano—playing the notes either separately or together—and then to ask the candidate to sing, or name, one of the notes, or alternatively, to state

---

[1] In criticism of this point of view Seashore (136), **App. p. i**, says: 'No credible test of musical talent can be built on this theory.'

the interval gap between them. If the candidate be asked to name one of the notes, the name of the other is always given.

Schoen (128) and Révész (123, 124), who were interested in the individual testing of children known to be musical, made use of a test of this nature.

The test was included in the present series as No. 13, where it has been modified for group purposes by using the same reference note throughout the test. Three forms were given; these were, in order of difficulty:

(a) Playing the two notes separately and asking the subject to give the name of the top note, when he had been told the name of the bottom one.

(b) Playing the notes together and asking the name of the top note, when the name of the bottom one had been given.

(c) Playing them together and asking the name of the bottom note, when the name of the top one had been given.

The tonic sol-fa names, the letter names, or the names of the intervals were all accepted as correct answers.

The performance of this task requires a certain amount of acquired knowledge which is, however, not greater than is often expected of young children.[1] However, it is preferable in psychological work to remove, as far as possible, any factors which might help a child who had had favourable opportunities. Moreover, it is often desired intended to apply the tests to adults, who quickly lose touch with these elementary technicalities. Modified forms of the test have therefore been used by such workers as Chevais (28), Madison (93), Lundin (92), Van Briessen (12), Vidor (159), Mainwaring (94), Drake (32), Révész (123) and by Serejewski & Maltzew (139). In these, two intervals are usually struck and the child is asked whether they are the same or different; alternatively, for individual assessment, an interval is struck, and then a third single note; the child is then asked to sing a fourth note which will make an interval with the third similar to that between the first two. The comparison of two intervals was used as a group test as No. 18 of my own series.

2. *Chord Analysis.* The Chord is, of course, an extension of the simple interval, and some of the Musicians' tests on chords are similar to those on intervals. Thus a test frequently used is one where a chord is struck, and the examinee asked to sing either the notes comprising it, or a given part, e.g. the alto, or bass. In more advanced examinations questions may be asked on the type of chord, its position (root, first, or second inversion), or the names of the notes may be required when one of them is given. Révész (124) showed that a musical prodigy on whom he used this test had considerable powers of analysing complex chords, and it was similarly used by Schoen (128) on musical children.

In order to adapt the test on chord analysis so that it would be suitable as a group test which would not involve acquired knowledge, it was modified in Test No. 1, where a chord was played, and the subject asked merely to state the number of notes. Both discords and various positions of the common chord were used.

---

[1] It was suggested in a musical journal that the child should be sufficiently familiar with notation to be able to answer this type of question by the age of 7 years. My own opinion is that this is rather too early an age for the average child.

The musical procedure of asking a child to sing a note from a chord was reversed for group purposes by playing a note, and then a chord, and asking the subject to state whether the note was in the chord or not; this is Test No. 11.

3. *Cadences*. This is the use of two successive chords to produce an effect of full or partial completion. The naming and detection of cadences has long been used in practical musical examinations.

A test on cadences was first employed as a psychological test by Lowery (88). As he pointed out, an ability to detect cadences should be important, because the subdivision of music into phrases, sentences, and sections is a 'punctuation' largely achieved by the use of cadences. The performer must indicate these cadences, and the listener must notice them, consciously or unconsciously, if the musical structure is to be made clear. I fully agree with Lowery on their importance, although whether they retain this sufficiently, when divorced from the accompanying music, to be used as a diagnostic test can only be discovered by checking the results from the use of such a test against an exterior criterion.

In Test No. 8 there are twenty items, in each of which two cadences are played,[1] and the subject is asked to state which gives the greater feeling of finality. The use of the dominant seventh has been avoided, since, although it is a great aid in defining the key (a matter of considerable importance with cadences), the examinee is likely to confuse the satisfied feeling of a properly resolved discord with the finality feeling of a perfect cadence. For children (and for some adults too) melody is of greater importance than harmony, and therefore the melodic line of the two cadences contained in any given item was made as similar as possible. All the usual variants on the cadence form have been employed, including inverted and root positions of chords in both the major and the minor modes.

4. (*a*) *The Resolution of Discords*. A discord is a chord which is not some variant of the common major or minor chord. Discords have been used as one of the chief harmonic interests in music from the time of Palestrina, and there has been an increasing tendency since Wagner to use them both unprepared and unresolved. The latter may be considered unpleasant by some people, others would hold a very different opinion. However, whether they are considered pleasant or the reverse, musicians in general would agree that discords give a more restful effect if they are properly prepared and resolved.

Owing to their harmonic importance discords frequently form the subject of aural tests where questions on whether a discord is resolved, its type, position, and so on are asked, or in written tests where the correct and artistic use of discords is assessed. The psychological tests on this subject, e.g. by Seashore (137), Van Briesson (12), and Stumpf (149) usually hinge on a comparison between degrees of dissonance or consonance.

Valentine (156) has shown that very young children make no distinction between

---

[1] The music is not that originally used by Lowery since his contains some slips in musical grammar. Thus, the doubling of the notes of the chords is sometimes incorrect, and in general the spacing of the chords is not that recommended by the text-books; the leading note often falls instead of rising, and the trebles are not arranged to be as nearly similar as possible.

discords and concords, but that powers of discrimination develop by about 12 years. It might follow as a corollary from these results that the capacity to distinguish the effects of discords should be indicative, in some measure, of a moderately advanced (over 12 years old) state of musical ability. If so, a test based on discord effects would be worth investigating.

In Test No. 9, 'discords played in their correct context (this gives a restful, satisfied effect) are contrasted with the same discords played in contexts which do not give this effect. The child is not asked which he prefers, for he may prefer the less usual without being in the least unmusical, but is asked to state which leaves him with the more restful feeling. The discords used included dominant sevenths, ninths, elevenths, thirteenths, with their inversions; augmented and diminished triads, augmented French, Italian and German sixths; suspensions, and six-four chords. In some cases the 'less restful' one is unresolved; in others it is unprepared, struck against its resolution, or resolved in an unusual manner.

(b) *Timbre*. A great deal of the variety of an orchestral performance comes. from the use of instruments of various timbres, and the ability to detect this variety must obviously add to the richness of the musical experience. In musical examinations it is assumed that this ability comes as a matter of experience and it is, as far as I am aware, never used as the subject of aural questions, although the correct and artistic use of instrumentation does form part of musical writing in the more advanced examinations.

Seashore has substituted a timbre test for his original test of consonance, and the mode of using it makes it almost one of discords, for the normal harmonic series approximates to the dominant thirteenth chord. The test is to decide the relative intensity of the third and the 'eleventh'[1] that is preferred, and according to this preference the subject's musical ability is assessed. It is open to doubt whether or not this will prove to be a good diagnostic test, because timbre quality is largely a matter of personal taste in which the musical child is as likely to choose the unusual as the usual.

Timbre had been previously used by Lowery(90) as a test of the capacity to attend to musical stimuli. In this test short musical phrases are played by two or more instruments (in ensemble) and the subject is asked to identify the instruments. The test, being one of recognition, is likely strongly to favour the child who has heard any quantity of orchestral music. In an attempt to avoid the effects of such opportunity Lowery gave the children a preliminary training in the identification of the separate instruments. In my opinion this training would have to be an extended one in order to make the investigator fairly sure that the child who had heard very little orchestral music was not at a great disadvantage compared with others who came from musical homes. Such extended training necessary as a preliminary greatly detracts from its use as a group test. For this reason, and because it is thought that the test on chord analysis already assesses the fundamental process required in the recognition of timbre, no test on timbre was included in my own tests.

[1] Seashore's fourth is equivalent to the eleventh of the dominant thirteenth chord.

5. *Key.* It is true that in the more modern music the writing tends to be atonal. However, these compositions probably depend for their effects upon the fact that the listener is key-conscious. In normal music the key of any particular section is usually well defined, and the variations of key that are introduced contribute considerably to the beauty of a composition by adding a sense of movement, through the change of position of the tonal centre.

As a realization of the key notes and of key changes is of such importance in music it is natural that it should form a frequent topic in music examinations, where a melody, with or without harmony, is sometimes played, and the candidate asked to sing the key note; or alternatively, after being given the original key, to state the changes that occur. In written papers the harmonization of a melody is a common question, and this implies, as a first step, a decision concerning the keys through which the melody passes.

The first of these three tests on key has been used by Kühn[78] to trace the growth of tonality in children. Reimers[121], who was interested in the same problem, asked the child to sing one song, and then to follow it by another. He noted whether the child took up the second song in the same key; if he did he assumed that the child had a developed sense of tonality. In another test Reimers altered the key of a few bars of a song and asked the child to locate the change. Both of these interesting tests are, of course, individual tests and not suitable for group assessment.

Although ability to detect a key change had not previously been used as a group psychological test of musical ability, it seemed to have possibilities of being a good test, for it is reasonable to suppose that a person who could detect such a change would be likely to be in a position to appreciate the changes which occur in actual music. A test was therefore compiled (No. 10) in which a short piece was played, and the subject asked to state whether it ended in the same key as that in which it began. In only a few items was there more than one change of key, and chromatic chords have been avoided. The music consisted of songs, hymns and chord progressions. The last were included as they allowed the test items to be considerably shorter than was possible with actual compositions.

The use of the word 'key' is not common among children, but the terms 'scale' and 'doh', together with the notion of 'movable doh', are taught in most schools by the time the children are 8 years old. An explanation of the meaning of the word 'key' was therefore added to the instructions as follows: 'If the key is different, then the doh is moved to a different place, or notes different from those used in the scale at the beginning of the piece of music have been added.'[1]

It was found advisable to give a few illustrations of the kind of answer required by using sections of the tunes of *God Save the King*, *The Bluebells of Scotland*, *Cherry Ripe*, *Who is Sylvia?*, and *Onward Christian Soldiers*, to illustrate the problem.

6. *Time Pattern Dictation.* There is considerable confusion in the precise meaning attached to the term 'rhythm' in music, and the question is more fully

---

[1] It is realized that as a general definition this might be considered weak, had chromatic chords been used in the selections; but these were avoided.

discussed under that heading on p. 25. I would agree with Mursell when he states that 'a musico-rhythmic response cannot be said to have been set up, unless tonal elements are present.'(107) In cases where a problem set is dealing merely with tapped patterns without relation to any tonal structure, it would appear preferable to use some other term than rhythm.[1]

If such a pattern is tapped out, it is a pattern in the intervals of time that elapse between the taps, and so it appears to me to be reasonable to call it a 'time-pattern' and to confine the term 'rhythm' to its use, in accordance with the custom among expert musicians, for 'the forward flow of music'.

In musical examinations the dictation of a tapped time-pattern is frequently used as a test of facility with notation. In my opinion the capacity to accomplish problems of this type which are not connected with tonal changes plays only a minor role in musical ability, for it appears frequently to be present in those of very small general musical capacity.

Many psychologists in the past have used either straightforward dictation of a time-pattern or some modification of it designed to overcome the difficulties of notation. Such tests (usually called rhythm tests) have been used by Seashore (133), Seashore, R. (131), Krone (76), Vidor (159), Schoen (128), Révész (123), Mainwaring (94) and Lowery (90). They have, as a rule, taken the form of comparing two patterns which are either tapped or given out on a buzzer, and the examinees are asked to say whether the two are the same or not. In some cases they have been asked to compare them with those existing in a piece of poetry or in musical phrases. With Lowery's test, the two patterns are given out in association with tones; Lowery rightly designated his test as one of 'time', for the task set is the comparison of two time-patterns where a consideration of the melodic shape does not enter into the problem.

An exercise in writing down a tapped time-pattern was used in the present series as No. 24. An attempt was made to lessen the notational difficulties by accepting answers in either staff, tonic sol-fa, musical shorthand, or some words which matched the commoner sound patterns used in music, e.g. London for two crotchets, Manchester for a crotchet and two quavers and so on.

7. *Musical Dictation.* Musical dictation has always been regarded by most music teachers as a searching test of musical ability and knowledge.

In psychology, various tests based on the reading or writing of notation have been employed. Most of these are concerned mainly with attainment, and are, therefore, really outside the scope of this work, which is on capacity. However, some of the best known are those by Roe (125), Knuth (71), Krone (76), Wright (171) and Torgerson & Fahnestock (152).

To lessen the attainment aspect, in some tests, e.g. of Kwalwasser & Dykema (82) and More (102), an adaptation is used in which a written tune is given; this is

---

[1] It is unfortunate that there is this confusion between the part (here designated 'time patterns') and the whole (rhythm), and that this confusion often extends to those with musical experience. It has been suggested by Cyril Winn that the double use of the term has now become so well established that it is unwise to try to confine the use of the word rhythm to its fullest meaning, and he has used the term 'rhythm' (spelt with a small 'r') for what are here designated 'time patterns', and 'Rhythm' for the whole forward flow of the music.

incorrect in some particulars, and the subject is asked to state where such inaccuracies occur. This last test would undoubtedly favour the child who had been fortunate enough to hear a large number of songs, or who had had considerable practice with notation, e.g. in learning to play an instrument.

In my own dictation test (No. 23) twenty graded melodies were played, and either tonic sol-fa or staff notation were accepted in answer. The subjects were instructed to neglect the time aspect of notation, as this had already been dealt with (in Test No. 6, which is mentioned above). The test was found to be too difficult for young children, and two attempts were made to simplify it. In the first (Test No. 22), in order to eliminate to a large extent the speed and memory factors, the National Anthem was used, and to make it still easier, the name of the first note in each phrase was given. In the second (Test No. 12), in order still further to reduce the difficulties of notation, the subjects were provided with the notation that was correct, except for the pitch of one or more notes. They were then asked to mark with a cross the first note that was incorrectly played.

Any form of musical dictation which involved the use of even quite ordinary harmony would be far too difficult for the average person, but two aspects of the problem, namely, chord memory and the ability to follow a moving part, were tested (in No. 2) by changing one note in any part of two successive chords, and asking the subject to state whether the direction of movement was up or down or if the two chords were the same. (This test was, in basic principle, very similar to one previously used by More (102).) The questions were of varying grades of difficulty, depending on the number of notes in the chord and on the position of the changed notes. A very similar test, containing only three part chords, in which the problem was to state which part moved, was also used (Test No. 19), as well as a variant of this in which sections from actual compositions were played (No. 19 a).

8. *Recognition of Music.* In a number of musical examinations the candidate must satisfy the examiners that he is acquainted with a considerable volume of music by naming the source of either written or played excerpts.

A similar test has been used in psychological work by Krone (76), Kwalwasser (81), Kwalwasser & Ruch (83), and Gildersleeve (47), in the form of recognizing music which is played or in notation.

This type of test has been used in No. 21, in which twenty songs were played and the examinees asked to give the title, a line, or just a few words to show that they had identified the melody.

9. *Memory.* Owing to the dynamic character of music, memory is a great aid in all musical activities. Thus all the tests so far mentioned have almost certainly involved musical memory to a considerable degree. In performers' examinations and in musical competitions the performer is usually rated a little higher if the composition is played from memory, and in some few examinations a test on the immediate recall of a played fragment is included.

Psychologists also have fully recognized the importance of memory; thus Drake (35) states that it is the primary factor in musical ability, and there are a variety of tests in existence. Seashore's well-known test has already been described.

Belaiew-Exemplarsky (5), Lowery (89), and Van Briessen (12) have all used the recognition of a tune in its variation form as a test of memory; this test may bring in other factors besides memory to a considerable degree; thus it probably involves general intelligence. Van Briessen (12), Drake (32), Lundin (92) and Brehmer (10) have employed some form of tune comparison, in which the subject states whether two melodies are the same or different. Singing back a dictated tune, after one or more auditions, has been used by Révész (123), Brehmer (10), Gordon (48), and Serejewski & Maltzew (139), as well as by Mainwaring (95) in an investigation on kinaesthesia; this test is, of course, only suitable for individual application. Mainwaring (94) also used questioning on the details of played or familiar tunes.

Of these tests mentioned, Seashore's appeared to me to be the best group test of memory.[1] However, it was felt that it would be improved by making the material approximate more closely to melodies. This change, although small, is nevertheless thought to be important, for the following reasons:

(a) The test then approaches more closely to the task required in dealing with actual music; it may reasonably be assumed that the closer the correspondence, the more likely are the results to be indicative of musical capacity.

(b) It has been shown by Gordon (48) that to the unmusical even melodies are nonsense material. It is in the awareness of the relations between the notes that a musician is marked off from the non-musician; if these relations are not present in any great degree, the musician has less opportunity to demonstrate his superiority.

(c) If, as in Test No. 3, little tunes are used, it is found that the number of notes can be easily increased to ten, and that these may be played far more quickly. This increase in tune length decreases the chance score, and so improves the reliability; the increase in speed means that the test will take less time, and this is helpful in building up an extended battery.

(d) A melodic line is far more interesting to those of high musical capacity than a haphazard collection of tones; they therefore co-operate better with the testing because their musical interests have been aroused.

10. *General Musical Knowledge.* One paper on general musical knowledge, form, notation, musical history and so on is often set in musical examinations.

Psychologists, too, have used such attainment tests, of which the best known are those by Gildersleeve (47) and Kwalwasser (81). A similar test was incorporated in the present series as No. 20. Most of the material used is likely to have been taught in school by the age of 12 years.

A general questionnaire was also included (No. 26) to throw light on the subject's instrumental training, interest, opportunity to hear music, parental musical interest, and so on. This was in order to try to estimate the effect of these factors on performance in the tests. Thus used as a means of giving broad classifications, and general indications of causes, the questionnaire is certainly useful, but for estimating the capacity to perform a task it would not appear to be sufficiently reliable for scientific purposes, and Mjöen (100) seems to have taken the technique

---

[1] Of all his tests this one has, according to the literature, been found to give the highest validity coefficient.

rather further than is legitimate in using it to estimate the ability of his subjects to improvise and sing a lower part to a melody.

Ability Tests not included in Musical Examinations, but used by Psychologists.

11. *Pitch.* (*a*) *Absolute.* A person is said to have absolute (perfect) pitch when he is able to give the name of any note which is played or sung, without having recently heard any reference note or chord; the name asked for is usually the letter name of the staff notation, but Wedell (161) has used the frequency instead. In true absolute pitch the answer is immediate and without reference to any conscious standard. Many people can make a fairly good guess at tuning their instrument, or at the name of a note, by mentally singing some notes as a reference point, e.g. the first note of *God Save the King* or the tuning note of their instrument. If the latter method of finding the pitch be excluded, perfect pitch would appear to be rare and fairly sharply defined, but if it is included, not only would perfect pitch be more common, but also it would be a less defined ability. This difference of definition would probably account for Maltzew's conclusion (96) that perfect pitch is fairly widespread, and according to the normal distribution curve. Many people including Boggs (9), Meyer (98), Mull (103), Petran (119), Gough (49) and Wienert (162) claim that it can be acquired, or is improved by practice; here they are probably dealing with those cases in which a reference note is being used.

A very few musicians regard perfect pitch as a valuable gift. However, discussion of the subject with many experienced teachers and musicians, including some who possessed it, gives the general impression that, although it is of some advantage in simple score reading, and in taking down dictated music, in other circumstances, such as transposing, playing or reading notation for a transposing instrument, or playing on an instrument that is not exactly at the pitch to which one is accustomed, it may be a distinct handicap, as the actual sounds do not correspond to those that are expected. Boggs (9), Schoen (128) and Révész (124) believe that the ability is an indication of general musical capacity, but some of their methods allow a certain amount of reference to be made. After experimental work on the subject, Vidor (159), Maltzew (96), von Kries (75) and Kohler (74) conclude that it is of little or no practical utility. This is in agreement with my own views and accordingly no test on this ability was included.

(*b*) *Relative Pitch.* The tests on relative pitch of Seashore (133) and of Kwalwasser & Dykema (82) (down to $\frac{1}{2}dv$ difference), and also the slightly wider one of Vidor (159) (2*dv*), would not appear to be of high diagnostic value when judged by the available experimental evidence. Mainwaring (94), on the other hand, based his test on the notes of the scale. Lundin (92) describes a test of melodic and harmonic transpositions and sequences, which I would regard as one mainly on relative pitch, as it hinges on the recognition of a musical pattern at a different pitch. In the case of my own tests, sensitivity to pitch relationships is the principal factor involved in Test No. 2, on stating the direction of movement of a part, and also in Tests 19 and 19 (*a*), all of which have already been described (page 20).

CHAPTER V

PSYCHOLOGICAL TESTS OF APPRECIATION

The psychological tests which have been mentioned, although they include practically all the methods that have so far been used to assess general musical capacity, have not involved any obvious assessment of the fundamental quality that all musicians would desire to find in any person who claims to have an interest in the art—namely, appreciation. It has been tacitly assumed by many workers that appreciation would be associated with ability to perform the type of test which uses elementary material, but this has yet to be proved.

It is to be expected that the attention of psychologists would be first given to the simpler aspects of music, since they present fewer difficulties of measurement than those of appreciation. So difficult is the latter that I have been seriously criticized for attempting to assess the immeasurable qualities of musical aesthetics.

The earliest account of an attempt to measure powers of appreciation appears to be that of Trabue (154), based on work by Mohler, who asked his examinees to assess the relative merit of gramophone records, in groups of three or four. His investigation merits more attention than it normally receives, although, considered as a standardized group test, it suffers from certain weaknesses. Unfortunately, as he used a collection of commercial records that are now out of circulation, it was not possible exactly to repeat his experiment and so to make use of the results which he obtained.

The experiment was, however, repeated with a new set of records. When an attempt was made to collect suitable records, difficulties in the method became apparent. If it be assumed that the four pieces of music, and not their actual performance, are to be compared, then the four records in one item should be played by the same or very similar orchestras. It would be unfair to have the good music played by a good orchestra and the poorer music played by an inferior band, but this is normally the case on gramophone records, so that it is practically impossible to get a series of four well-graded pieces played by similar orchestras.

A number of records, selected after some difficulty, was played to a group of 45 school-children. The results seemed influenced by little else than chance because, as questioning showed, the children found the comparison of four records too difficult, as they had forgotten the first record by the time the fourth was played. The series was improved by reducing the number of records in each item to two. The problem was still too difficult, mainly because, as the children put it, they 'did not quite know what they were looking for, and so guessed'. An item analysis of the results showed that if any record happened to be known, it was immediately preferred, irrespective of its musical merits. A practical objection to the test was that even if only a section of each record was played, the test took more time to apply than could be spared for a single test.

Although the general principle of Mohler's work appears, on musical grounds, to be excellent, the results showed that modifications were necessary, chiefly in the direction of simplifying the test. Even a judge at a musical competition does not have such a complicated task as that mentioned above; it is indeed doubtful whether an expert would care to undertake the assessment of performances in which both the merits of the pieces played and of their performance by different orchestras had to be evaluated on one general scale. It is true that in some festivals the candidates are allowed to choose their own music, but the judgement is based on the performance and not on the piece chosen; again, when orchestral performances are being assessed, the orchestras are graded into classes. The judge thus takes a more limited field for comparison than that set by Mohler. For the untrained person the field must be made more limited still. This can be done by asking him to direct his attention to one aspect of the music at a time, e.g. the harmony, or phrasing.

I have already raised objections to the dissection of the elements of music away from their musical content, and it might be thought that it is here proposed to follow the same procedure. However, the elements were not removed from the general musical structure, but the examinee was merely asked to turn his attention to some specified factor in two performances he was required to compare. These features were some which were easily identified by a person untrained in musical technicalities, and no attempt to identify the changes that had taken place was asked for, but the process was based on preference or taste.

Besides simplifying the problem for the listener, if the music is thus divided into sections which deal with one aspect at a time, the results will allow an investigation into the following points:

 (a) In what order these separate aspects develop in the child.
 (b) Which are lacking in the musically backward.
 (c) Whether the aspects are evenly distributed in a given person. This may be of importance in indicating a handicap in a particular direction in a child who is otherwise a promising candidate for training.[1]

The process used is similar to that employed with success by Bulley (15) in estimating the ability to appreciate pictorial art, in which the subject is asked to arrange a number of pictures in order of merit, and then the choice made is compared with that of the expert. If the pictures from which to choose are shown in pairs, the person who guesses blindly will get half of them right by chance, and at the other end of the scale, few are likely to get them all correctly placed. This gives a narrow field of marks which tends to reduce the reliability. It is therefore desirable to give as wide a choice as possible by giving a number to rank, and this is easily done in pictorial art, where the specimens may be inspected at leisure and a considered judgement given. Music, however, presents more difficulties, for by its nature it is intangible and dynamic, and the effects produced are fleeting; moreover, most people have poor memories for music, so that they can make but

[1] If there should prove to be a strong general factor in musical ability the last remarks will not be so applicable, but in that case the sections will help to indicate the existence of a general factor, or to check the truth of any hypothesis, such as that of Seashore, in which he states that 'music is a hierarchy of talents, many of which are independent'.

little use of a delayed judgement based on the auditory images. These considerations made it advisable to employ only short sections of music, and to present a choice from two only. The marks obtainable by guessing were reduced to one-third of the total by including some items in which the two performances were the same. After hearing the two selections the examinee decides whether they are the same or different; in the former case he writes down 'S', or in the latter case he states his preference, writing 'A' for the first version or 'B' for the second.

At the time when this investigation was commenced there was little published work on the subject of tests of musical appreciation. Apart from the experiment of Mohler's, mentioned above, there were some investigations by Vernon on the choice of a programme, and by Adler and Hevner, in which an original and one or more versions that had been mutilated in ways not specified to the subject, were presented for choice. In addition work had also been carried out by Burt, while engaged on the problems of vocational guidance at the National Institute of Industrial Psychology. Beyond a brief mention of the tests [17] and some of the results, it has unfortunately not been published. I have been concerned with the appreciation of music as actually composed and performed by musicians. Other workers, notably Drake, Kwalwasser and Dykema, Lowery, Schoen, and Vidor have attacked the problem by the use of specially written music. Their tests are discussed below under the heading of the aspects of appreciation which they were investigating.

There have been some tests published since by Hevner & Landsbury, and also some by Semeonoff on an isolated aspect of musical appreciation. Both the Oregon tests of Hevner and Landsbury and my own appreciation tests are a development of those of Mohler and of Adler. Adler [1] used six items in each of which an original composition, chosen as a fine specimen of music, was compared with three mutilated versions made 'dull', 'chaotic' or 'sentimental' by alterations in the melody, harmony and rhythm; the subject was then asked to choose the best and worst of each four and his choice compared with that of the experts. Hevner [59, 60] modified the procedure to make it somewhat simpler and in the Oregon tests (Hevner and Landsbury [61]) there are forty-eight paired items in which the original, and a version mutilated in either rhythm, harmony or melody, are played; the subject then states both his preference and also in which of these aspects the mutilation occurs—in six cases the mutilation is in more than one aspect. The Oregon test scores are not standardized in norms, but in percentile ranks for College students.

A fuller discussion of the appreciation tests is given below:

12. *The Appreciation of Rhythm.* The word rhythm is derived from the Greek ρυθμός which means 'measured motion'. The critic or advanced musician uses it in this manner, to convey the realization of the idea of movement towards points of climax and repose.[1] As music can hardly be said to exist without tonal variation, musical rhythm can only truly be said to be present when it is associated with

---

[1] This is, no doubt, the sense in which the term is used by Seashore [136] when he discusses rhythm; but in the title of his test it is used for what I have designated 'time pattern'.

tones, and the term will be so used in the present work. Rhythm in music is mainly conveyed by the tune shape (which also implies cadence points), the style of time used (e.g. 6/8 or 4/4) and the accenting of certain important notes in the melody.

This use of the word rhythm in music is parallel to its use in other arts. In poetry rhythm is the general effect of the flow of the words, and metre is one of the means by which it is achieved. In painting, it is used to denote how far the separate parts produce a feeling of contribution to a harmonious climax in the picture. In ballet dancing, it is used for the larger movements, with their rise and fall, which are more nearly related to the melodic shape of the music than the beats and smaller time-patterns. So also in eurhythmics it is applied to the arm or general bodily movements of the child rather than for marching in time to the accent.

A problem on rhythm which is sometimes set in musical examinations is to give the candidate a written unbarred melody, and request him to insert the correct bar lines. To do this he must examine the general shape of the tune and decide which notes should be emphasized so that an easy flow is assured towards the correct point of climax. As part of the problem he has to decide which is the most appropriate time (e.g. 3/8, 6/8, 9/8 or 12/8); the bar lines have then to be so placed that the important notes come at the beginning of the bar and receive the correct accentuation.[1] This problem I would designate as a true test of rhythm, and not merely of time-pattern, as the fundamental consideration is the general melodic shape. For the group testing of those who have little or no technical training, two methods of barring the same melody are played in Test No. 4, and the subject is asked to state his preference.

The Oregon tests also include items in which the original composition is contrasted with a version mutilated in rhythm, this time by abrupt changes in time signature. It may be seen that my own and the Oregon tests differ, in that in the former the contrast is between two different rhythms and in the latter between a good one and one which is abruptly changed from time to time.

13. *The Appreciation of Melodic Shape.* The most important features which distinguish a good melody from a poor one are probably to be found in the shape of the general tonal curve, and in the variety and the balance of interval progressions, of time groups, of phrases and counterphrases, and of keys. The proper interplay of these factors will mean that the progressions to points of climax and repose will be satisfactory.

In advanced musical examinations the capacity to appreciate these points is shown in free composition, and in more elementary examinations by questions on the completion of a melody of which the first phrase is given, or in which there is a choice between two given endings. These questions may also be set in practical examinations in which the student is required to sing or to play the answer.

This test has been used by Schoen (128), Kwalwasser and Dykema (82), Vidor (159) and by Drake (32). Lowery (90) gives a test, which he designates a creation test, in

---

[1] The possible choice of incorrect answer is wider than might at first be apparent, and even composers have incorrectly barred some of their own music. For example, Chopin's Nocturne in E flat, which has been barred as 12/8, might be more appropriate as 6/8.

which the subject is asked whether a phrase is suited to a preceding one—the answer to be a 'Yes' or 'No'. This test would appear to me to be one on the appreciation of melodic shape rather than on creative ability.

In the present tests the principle has been adopted that only music which is generally considered good by musicians is to be used as a standard of reference. If this principle were followed in the present case and a choice given between a good tune and one that had been altered, then acquaintance with the melody would be of great assistance, and the subject who had had favourable opportunities would be greatly helped. For this reason the choice given was not between an original and a mutilated version, as in the Adler[1] and Oregon tests[61], but between two different melodies (Test No. 15). An effort was made to obtain pairs of tunes which were comparable in general shape, key, pace, time and character, but this was difficult. Gernet[44] has used a somewhat similar procedure with themes.

In the case of this test it is possible to obtain a procedure similar to the ranking of a large number of works of pictorial art by omitting the playing, as in Test No. 16, where ten familiar tune titles were given to rank in order of preference. This gave a test which is in many respects very similar to that applied to adults by Vernon[158], who asked them to compile, from a given list, the programme they would most like to hear. In both Vernon's and my own the choice made was afterwards compared with that of the general opinion of the experts.

14. *The Appreciation of Harmony.* Melody and Harmony are very closely related. Thus many melodies may be regarded as variations of the treble in a simple chord progression, and also a melody will often immediately suggest a suitable harmony to accompany it. The harmony is an integral part of the musical structure, and not, as it is sometimes regarded by the unmusical, a mere addendum to the tune; its appreciation is an important part of the appreciation of the whole composition.

In most advanced musical examinations the candidate is expected to be able to harmonize a melody, or to construct a suitable chord progression on a given bass. Answering such questions involves a considerable measure of taste in the selection of the chords, or in the construction of the melody. Such a question obviously demands a well-developed knowledge of acquired musical technicalities and, for this reason, needs considerable adaptation if it is to be used as a group test. In the very interesting psychological tests on harmony by Kwalwasser[79], a number of short chord progressions, each consisting of three chords, are played, and the subject is asked to state whether each progression is good or bad. In my own test (No. 25), two chord progressions are presented, but the number of chords has been extended beyond three to a number sufficient to define clearly the key. The use of only three chords in the progressions tends to leave the key somewhat ambiguous and this influences the correctness or otherwise of the progression. Music is primarily a matter of note relationships, which remain uncertain unless the key is firmly established.

I have, for various reasons, been concerned to make my tests as musical as possible, and so a more musical variant of the harmony test (No. 5) was devised; in this a fine harmonic example, taken from classical music, was compared with a reharmonized version. This test contains more aspects of harmony than can be included in a simple block chord progression—such things as sequences and contrapuntal melodies. The items are arranged to give a wide range of difficulty, so that inability to appreciate the difference between the easiest examples may be taken to be almost a zero appreciation of harmony as it occurs in actual music, while the difficult examples tax the power of an accomplished musician. Adler[1] used a somewhat similar method in which selections of music were compared, and among these were some mutilated in harmony, although this was not the only mutilation in any single item. To obtain standard delivery he used a pianola, whilst I used specially prepared gramophone records. Hevner & Landsbury[61], in tests published after this investigation was commenced, followed Adler's procedure in the manner already described.

15. *Appreciating the Fitness of a Composition.* One of the characteristics of good music is its fitness for the intended purpose. In musical examinations the candidate may be asked to write a short section for a given purpose, e.g. a chorale or a setting for a poem, and for a degree examination he is normally asked to submit a longer work, such as a complete song, or a quartet. In such cases the candidate would be penalized, no matter how academically correct his writing, if the style of the composition were not fitting to its particular purpose.

In psychological work, there have been a number of investigations where the process has been reversed and the subject asked to give his reactions to music. Thus, Gundlach[52] asked his subjects to choose from a list the mood word which best described the composition. Also, since this work was commenced, an account of a test, on lines very similar to my own, has been published by Semeonoff[138]. The two tests are very much alike; in each a short selection of music is played and a choice of titles is given (three in the present case in Test No. 14), and the examinee is asked to select the one which he would regard as the most fitting. In the case of my own tests, the choice was thought to be indicative of musical capacity if it coincided with that of the composer.

It is in connection with the music used for the test that differences of opinion are likely to arise. Semeonoff prefers to use music which purports to suggest definite pictures; my own opinion is that music cannot, in the main, suggest such pictures except by fortuitous associations, but that it can suggest emotional states—including feelings of rest or movement. If this latter hypothesis be accepted, the best pieces of music for this test are those which have a mood title such as 'Joy', 'Sorrow', 'Anguish', 'Hope', or those which provoke emotions, such as 'A Soldiers' March', 'Death Song', 'Night Fantasies' and 'Happy Shepherd'. A few qualities—chiefly of movement—were also used, such as 'Shimmering water', with a quickly moving motif; 'Catch me if you can', also with very rapid movement; 'Giant motif', with very slow and heavy chord movement. It is not, of course, suggested that the music forms a picture of the giant or other object in the mind of the listener, but that the music has certain qualities that would make its real title more appropriate than the other two given, and the test is designed to determine whether the subject can detect the presence of these qualities in the music.

16. *Creative Ability*. That early creative work is largely a rearrangement of past experience may be seen by an examination of the early compositions of most composers. Any test of innate creative ability should therefore take into account the child's musical experience, how far any tune bears marks of originality and how far it is taken directly from some melody previously heard. A test used by Vater (157) and Vidor (159) was to give the child a tapped time pattern on which he could build a tune. These tunes might possibly be sorted out into typical shapes, on similar lines to the drawings of a man done at various ages and intelligence levels (16). Such work could not be carried out as a group test, because the children have not the necessary notational facility to write down their efforts. Any test based on the choice of the better ending to a melody is one of taste in melody rather than of creation. After some consideration of the problem it was thought that, at the present stage in music testing, creation tests could only be carried out by individual methods, and even then only with great difficulty; they were regarded as beyond the scope of the present work on group tests of musical capacity.

17. *The Appreciation of Intensity Changes*. A musician would find it difficult to write down or perform music without some indication of the phrasing and intensity changes, for they form an integral part of the musical structure. They are the main methods by which music is 'interpreted', i.e. the musical shape made apparent to the listener, and, as such, are always carefully assessed in any advanced executants' examination. No hard and fast principles can be laid down concerning the relation between the musical structure and the use of crescendos and decrescendos, but as a general rule the intensity gets louder as a climax approaches and falls towards the anti-climaxes; also, a rising passage is more often associated with a crescendo than the reverse. It is an appreciation of the artistic use of intensity changes in tonal structures which marks a musician, who may be quite insensitive to such changes in other directions, e.g. in the use of the speaking voice.

The comparison of two intensities has been used by Seashore (133) and Kwalwasser & Dykema (82) in the manner already described. In these tests no account is taken of the relation between tonal structures and intensity change and, probably for this reason, that type of test has not been very successful.

In Test No. 6, selections from actual music are played with intensity changes that a musician would regard as satisfactory, and contrasted with others in which the intensity changes conflict with the structure of the melody. The problem is not merely to detect the changes, but also to decide which of the two is the more appropriate.

18. *The Appreciation of Good Phrasing*. Close attention is always paid by the critic or examiner to the correct execution of phrasing. The latter, which is recognized as an important part of musical interpretation, requires, for its proper performance, an understanding of the structure of the music, for phrasing is the division of the music into its logical groups and sections. It is indicated mainly by short pauses between the phrases; the pauses are not actually written as rests in the notation but are indicated by slurs above the music. In some instrumental music the phrasing indications may not, for various reasons, be fully indicated; thus, for

stringed instruments, the slurs correspond to the bowing and, as the length of the
bow is limited, they do not always indicate the full phrase. The pauses correspond
in general to the so-called breathing spaces in speech, in songs and in playing wind
instruments (although it is actually unnecessary to breath at the end of every
phrase). Phrasing is one of the components that go to make up rhythm, and has
the same relation to music as punctuation has to poetry and prose.

Amongst psychological writers, Mursell(107) would seem clearly to have assessed
it at its proper value, when he says: 'The analogy with language is very close. We
hear spoken language as sentences or phrases, i.e. meaningful units in sequence,
and not as a series of words or syllables; music is read in the same way.' Lowery (88)
has used a phrasing test which would appear to me to be more a test of memory
than of ability to divide music into appropriate sections. I have therefore already
included it under that heading. Hevner (60) has published an account of a test
which included items in which the original phrasing was incidentally disturbed by
changes in melody, harmony or rhythm, as was also the case with Adler's tests.

In my own phrasing test (No. 7) a well-phrased piece of music is contrasted with
a weaker version, and the subject asked to make a choice. As the phrasing is to
a large extent made apparent by the use of cadences, some of the more difficult
items are played without harmony, in which case the cadence is not actually
present to aid the subject. The term 'phrasing' is not a familiar one to children, but
the use in the instructions of the analogy with language was found to make the
task required easily intelligible.

19. *The Appreciation of the Correct Pace.* By altering the speed at which a phrase
is spoken a sentence may be changed from having a deep emotional significance to
a ridiculous one. A similar effect obtains in music. Although the pace which
various musicians prefer for a given work may vary slightly, the variations fall
within narrow limits. The pace is largely determined by the structure of the music,
being chiefly affected by the melodic shape and more especially by the harmonic
construction—thus a piece in rapid tempo will rarely have more than one chord to
a bar. An experienced conductor or performer will glance at the notation and,
without reference to the metronomic instructions, commence to play at almost the
pace indicated by the composer. When teaching young (and therefore comparatively undeveloped) performers, difficulties are often experienced in getting them
to exercise taste in the matter of tempo, unless they are exceptionally gifted. In
general, the use of the correct pace may be taken as one mark of a fairly advanced
stage in appreciation.

No previous psychological work appears to have used this aspect of music as the
basis of a test. In my own test (No. 17) the same selection is played at three
different metronome speeds, one of these being that indicated in a reliable edition
of the music. The examinee is then asked to state his preference. The playing was
not always taken in a fixed order, e.g. of slow, medium, fast, but other orders were
also used; this was because it was hoped to investigate the direction in which
misjudgements were most likely to occur, and it was desired to eliminate any
influence due to the order in which the slower or faster items were played.

20. *Form.* In certain advanced musical examinations the candidate is given the notation and asked various questions on the form (structure) of the composition. Often the candidate for a musical degree is required to submit an entire composition which must, of course, have a satisfactory form. Both of these tasks require too much acquired knowledge to be used as psychological group tests of musical capacity.

No specific test for form appears to exist in psychology. A method that suggested itself was to contrast two compositions whose forms were satisfactory and unsatisfactory respectively, and then to ask for a choice. This would, however, take too much time, as a fairly large section of music would need to be played. Any test involving the playing of a single piece, followed by questioning on the form of construction, would test memory, and perhaps intelligence, quite as much as capacity to appreciate form, and was not considered suitable. Owing to these difficulties no special test for form was included in the series.

One aspect of musical ability, which has not previously been mentioned, was quickly made apparent on obtaining the examinees' introspections, for the latter showed that many of the tasks set in the tests were solved by the use of auditory imagery. So common was this that it seemed to be redundant to design any special methods for separately assessing the capacity. Seashore[136] has attempted to measure the strength of auditory imagery by means of the subject's self-assessment on a questionnaire, but it is doubtful whether this technique can give sufficiently reliable results for making any quantitative estimate.

For the appreciation tests mentioned above a total of about 150 short selections of music were chosen, each being a good example of the particular aspect which it was desired to test. As these pieces were to be used as standards of reference, it was important that they should not be of doubtful quality. Considerable care was therefore taken in their choice. If a piece of music (*a*) were taken from the best work of expert composers, (*b*) were thought good by the consensus of musicians, (*c*) had survived the test of time and (*d*) were taken from a reliable edition, it was assumed that it would be representative of good art. As a check on personal views the selections were submitted to musical friends (too numerous to mention, but to whom I am none the less grateful) for their opinions, and any doubtful items were removed.

By thus using standard works for reference there was a grave risk of favouring the trained listener. However, preliminary experiments showed that the number of items known by the average child or adult was very small. Furthermore, it appeared preferable to take this risk, even if the test might later prove to be unsuitable for experienced musicians, rather than to be open to the still graver criticism of using an equivocal basis for the samples of good music. To mitigate any effect of using known compositions, the pieces were chosen from a wide range of vocal and instrumental music, and from the work of over thirty composers. Some traditional songs were added later. The range was also made a wide one in order not to favour a listener who had a predilection for a particular type of composer or music. Later investigations fully justified the use of music which might possibly be known.

The tests were written for the piano as being easily available to future workers, and because the instrument is familiar to children as their usual medium for school music lessons; this helps the children to settle down quickly to the tasks set. The practical needs of the music teacher, as well as the more theoretical aims, have been kept in view, and for them, especially, the piano is the most convenient means of giving the tests.

A table which summarizes the main tests that have been employed by musicians, and by the various investigators mentioned herein, is given at the end of this chapter. The full list of my own tests is also given below for ease of reference.

Tests used in the Preliminary Battery for this Investigation.

(a) *The Short Series* (applied by means of specially prepared gramophone records):

1. Detecting the number of notes played in a single chord; occasionally the 'chord' may consist of one note only.
2. Detecting and stating the direction of change of a single note in a repeated chord.
3. Detecting changes of notes in a short melodic phrase.
4. Judging the more appropriate rhythmic accentuation in two versions of the same melody.
5. Judging the more appropriate of two harmonizations of the same melody.
6. Judging the more appropriate mode of varying loudness (crescendo, decrescendo, etc.) in two versions of the same melody.
7. Judging the more appropriate phrasing (grouping of the notes by pauses, legato and staccato playing, slight under or over holding, etc.) in two versions of the same piece.

(b) *Additional Tests applied by Gramophone Records:*

8. Judging the more complete cadence.
9. Discriminating between resolved and unresolved discords.
10. Detecting a change of key.
11. Detecting the presence of a given played note in a chord.
12. Detecting an error of pitch in a played tune when compared with the notation.
13. Naming the top or bottom note of an interval.

(c) *Additional Tests applied by the Piano only:*

14. Judging which of three given titles would best describe the character of a played selection.
15. Judging the better of two played melodies.
16. Judging the order of merit of a given list of melodies.
17. Judging the best pace from three performances differing only in tempo.

18. Detecting whether or not two intervals are the same.
19. Detecting which line of the music is moving. Also detecting which line is moving most when more than one may be moving.
20. General musical knowledge questionnaire.
21. Recognizing played tunes.
22. Writing down the National Anthem from memory.
23. Writing down, from dictation, graded unknown melodies.
24. Writing down a 'time-pattern' (using staff, sol-fa, taa-tai, shorthand, or word notation).
25. Judging the better of two chord progressions.
26. A questionnaire on general musical interests, training, home music, etc.

Some preliminary work was carried out with twenty-one of the tests, by applying them to 271 school-children, aged 11–13 years (165). Five of the above tests had not then been devised, those which were not used being numbers 3, 15, 16, 18 and the questionnaire. At this early stage the tests each contained ten items, the range of music and composers was limited, and the choice was given between a good version and a weaker one (no pairs being played alike). A few adjustments were made after applying them to musical friends, but no further alterations were made after they were given to the first group of school-children. The main purpose of that investigation was to examine the possibilities of tests which used musical material, especially those that involved a measure of appreciation, rather than to derive a highly developed battery. Full details of this early work are given elsewhere (165); it may here be stated that it was sufficiently satisfactory to indicate that the approach had possibilities, and that useful results might be obtained by an extension of the work.

The results may be summarized as follows:

1. By getting a correlation of 0·64 with a teacher's ranking it showed that the type of test was likely to prove efficient, for this figure was considerably higher than any that had previously been reported.

2. Results with German and with English groups gave almost the same averages (for similar ages and corresponding schools), indicating that the results were not being unduly influenced by differences of environment, and that it was, therefore, more probable that an innate capacity was being assessed, rather than one based on opportunities.

3. The distribution curves obtained were sufficiently regular to show that correlation coefficients might be calculated.

4. A factor analysis of a group of 34 boys, using Thurstone's centroid method, showed a general factor, and also a second factor that appeared to divide the tests into two types, of which one was suggested as being analytical.

	By musicians	By psychological workers	By the Author
Ability type (detection)			
1	Intervals	Serejewski & Maltzew, Révész, Schoen, Drake, Mainwaring, Vidor, Chevais, Van Briessen, Lundin, Madison	13, 18
2	Chord analysis	Schoen, Révész	1, 11
3	Cadences	Lowery	8
4	Discords	Seashore, Valentine, Stumpf, Van Briessen	9
	(Timbre)	Seashore, Lowery	—
5	Key	Reimers, Kühn	10
6	Time pattern	Krone, Seashore, Révész, Schoen, Mainwaring, Vidor, Seashore, R., Lowery	24
7	Musical dictation	Krone, Wright, Kwalwasser & Dykema, Torgerson & Fahnestock, Roe, More, Knuth	12, 22, 23
8	Recognizing music	Kwalwasser & Ruch, Kwalwasser, Gildersleeve, Krone	21
9	Memory	Seashore, Lowery, Brehmer, Révész, Mainwaring, Drake, Belaiew-Exemplarsky, Van Briessen, Gordon, Serejewski & Maltzew, Lundin	3
10	General knowledge and other questionnaires	Kwalwasser, Seashore, Gildersleeve, Mjöen, Van Briessen, Copp	20
11	Pitch: (a) Absolute	Schoen, Révész, Wedell, Meyer, Boggs, Mull, Petran, Wienert, von Kries	—
	(b) Relative	Kwalwasser & Dykema, Seashore, Vidor, Mainwaring, More, Lundin	2, 19, 19a
Appreciation type (judgement)			
12	Rhythm	Hevner & Landsbury, Adler	4
13	Melodic shape including whole composition	Schoen, Lowery, Adler, Kwalwasser & Dykema, Vernon, Mohler, Vidor, Gernet, Hevner & Landsbury, Drake	15, 16
14	Harmony	Kwalwasser, Adler, Hevner & Landsbury	5, 25
15	Fitness	Semeonoff	14
16	Creative ability	Vidor, Vater	—
17	Intensity	Seashore	6
18	Phrasing	(Adler, Hevner)	7
19	Pace	—	17
20	Form	—	—

CHAPTER VI

THE DEVELOPMENT OF THE TEST MATERIAL

It was concluded from the preliminary work that the tests compiled would form a basis from which, after suitable development, a short battery could be derived that would be likely to satisfy the criteria adopted. Before passing judgement on any isolated test it was tried and repeatedly revised until its limitations and possibilities could be more clearly seen. In the earlier stages it was not possible to say whether any unsatisfactory results were due to the music used, or to the method of application, or whether it was inherent in the style of test under review.

For this part of the work 794 children, aged 11–16 years, were tested in school classes. These classes normally had an age range of only a few months, but sometimes included two or three who were a year older or younger than the average. As a result of this work it was possible to make about thirty adjustments to each test as groups became available.

It would be tedious to give the full details of the evolution of all the tests from their early stages up to the form in which they were standardized, but one—the test of harmony—will be discussed more fully, and the methods described may be taken to apply, in general, to the others.

The first step was to choose examples of straightforward harmony that were of considerable artistic merit; so ten of the Bach chorales were selected. This music makes use of all the generally known technique of that period, and by modern standards would be considered very full and rich, and as showing genius without being *outré*. Many musicians who spend the majority of their time in studying harmony regard them as the finest of their type, and as some of the best examples of harmony in any style. From the point of view of this investigation they were particularly suitable for the following reasons:

(a) They are meant to be played slowly, and this gives the subject time to grasp the significance of the chords.

(b) Their hymn-like nature makes them as familiar an idiom as any music is likely to be.

(c) They are free from any complicated or extreme examples of rhythm, ornamentation, enharmonic changes of key, or other musical factors that would be likely to cause dislike merely on account of their strangeness to a listener of narrow musical experience.

Each chorale was reharmonized after the style of Bach by the author. On completion, passing notes were added in similar places to those of the original in order to avoid the possibility that the subject might pass judgement on this factor instead of on the harmony. The new version was correct but dull harmony, and to an expert in harmony the difference between the original and reharmonized versions was considerable. The ten chorales, together with their reharmonized versions, were played in pairs to some musical friends, each pair being played twice; but the problem of distinguishing them was found to be too difficult for the average musician. The music was, therefore, revised by making some of the reharmonized versions weaker, until the most musical of the subjects could just manage to get them all right, and the rather less musical could solve the easier items without difficulty. The test was then given to a group of schoolboys aged 16 years; once more the task was found to be too difficult and again the gap between the original and reharmonized versions needed to be made wider for some of the items.

The ten complete chorales took a considerable time to play, so it seemed desirable to reduce the time by using only two phrases. In order to estimate the effect of such shortening, items of the tests were played in both the longer and in the shortened forms to a group of adults, who were asked to give their introspections. It appeared that comparison was more difficult when the long sections of music were employed, as the impression from the first had died away before the second was completed. A few of the subjects stated that they preferred the longer playing; they were apparently those who adopted a system of assessment of each version as they heard it. An attitude of comparison was, however, more common, and for the majority of listeners short pieces were therefore desirable.

The test in the shortened form was applied to a group of adolescents, and it was found that the coefficient of correlation with the results of the whole battery had improved. As there were so few items in the test this coefficient could not be regarded as very significant; nevertheless it did give a general indication that the shortened form was rather better.

This test was then applied to the groups of children mentioned at the end of the last chapter. The new data showed that the test was still too difficult for general application to children of about 11 years, even though the harmony of some of the poorer versions was so weak. Therefore, as fresh groups were tested, the difference between the two versions was made wider, by stages, until the present music for these chorales was reached.

It was thought that if the children were given familiar tunes which had contrasting accompaniments, they might then be better able to turn their attention away from the melody to the harmony. Some well-known folk-songs with good simple harmony were therefore selected, and each was contrasted with a version to which a weak harmony had been added. These folk-songs proved to be as difficult as the chorales and had to be made easier until the harmony finally depended almost entirely on one or two chords, and even these were nearly always incomplete, having the third or fifth, or both, missing from the chord. The result is thin, uninteresting, bad writing. Known tunes seemed to be just as difficult as unknown ones, a result that was later fully confirmed with a larger mass of experimental data. However, the children were definitely stimulated and interested when a known tune appeared and, as a result, gave greater attention to the whole test, so that a few of these items were retained in place of some of the Bach chorales.

The test was now in rather too homogeneous a state, being still too difficult for the young children and not difficult enough for the musical adult. Also, the small number of items so far used gave a narrow range of marks, and this tended to make the tests less reliable than was desired; so the ten items were increased to twenty. Five of as easy a type as could be devised were added (two-part harmony was in practice found much easier than three- or four-part) together with five difficult ones. The latter depended on chord progressions, sequential patterns and melodies in parts other than the treble, rather than on the construction of each chord. At the same time the number of playings was reduced from two for each item to one only. This was partly because it had already been observed that, for the majority of the examinees, the second playing was a waste of time, as they inserted their answers after the first playing, and partly because the time involved in playing so many tests twice made the children fatigued, and made the teachers and other authorities unwilling to sacrifice so many of their teaching periods.

It was thought that a given type of music might possibly favour certain listeners; for example, those who liked Bach chorales would probably be interested and likely to do better because of this than other listeners who preferred the romantic composers. The range of composers was therefore extended to cover periods up to comparatively modern styles. Jazz music was not included, as this would be unlikely to yield examples of really good harmony, would be likely to prejudice the authorities against the tests, and would waste the children's time if they were listening to poor music.

After many of the revisions, the order of difficulty was found by an item analysis, and some adjustments were made to get the items well spaced in difficulty, the easier ones being placed first. The difficulty depended more on the nature than on the number of the faults in the reharmonized version. These faults, placed roughly in the order of their detection, were:

1. Definitely harsh combinations, such as the fourth and the diminished fifth, replaced the softer thirds and sixths.
2. The chords were made thin by omitting the third or the fifth, or both, and using the octave instead.
3. The chords were made unbalanced by wrong doubling, e.g. of the third instead of the root.
4. There was a monotonous use of the same chord.
5. Harmonic interests, such as the seventh or the ninth, were absent.
6. The chord progressions were weak.
7. The progression of the parts was unmelodic.
8. Bass sequences were absent.

Up to this stage the choice had been between two versions, so that half marks could be obtained by guessing. By including four items in which the two versions were the same, the number of possible answers was increased to three, and the number of marks which could be gained by chance was thereby reduced. It was found that the tests were improved in reliability because of the resultant widening of the range of marks.

The introspections of some of the adult musicians showed that the announcing of the second version had a disturbing effect, in so far as it was an interrupting factor in separating the two sections of music which the listeners were comparing. This was therefore discontinued, and the versions were divided by a pause of three seconds. It was found that even with young children there was little danger of the subjects mistaking the second version for a continuation of the first.

The number of items in which 'A' or 'B' was the correct answer was, of course, the same; they were distributed in a 'random' order, and so that there was an even distribution of A's among the easy and the difficult questions. An item analysis was made, and the percentage of correct answers among the A's and the B's was calculated. It appeared that the B's had a slight advantage, so they were re-arranged in order to give more of the easy ones to the A's. A few examinees said, on introspection, that they felt that the B's would always have a slight advantage, for familiar music was preferred; thus, if they were doubtful of the correct answer, the B, being slightly better known, was selected. These comments are in agreement with the conclusions of Krugman (77) who found that familiarity breeds liking. However, the influence referred to was so slight, that it was considered that the effect could be ignored.

The item analysis further showed that some of the more modern music, for example, that of Ireland or even the music of Ravel or Wagner, was extremely difficult for children. These pieces of music were intended to be difficult items, and it was hoped that they would be effective in grading the more musical subjects. However, although the bottom 30 % in musical capacity (as judged on the results of the whole of the tests) secured only the chance total, as was expected, the top 30 % actually obtained less than this, and tended to prefer the bad item. These few items were therefore investigated by playing them to musical friends and obtaining their opinions and introspections. There was no doubt that these adults preferred the one intended, giving as their reasons that they found the better one 'interesting', 'original', 'out of the ordinary', 'rich', etc. A few listeners identified the style.[1]

The group of children was subjected to the test again and asked this time to give the reasons for their answers. Discussion showed that the better children had noticed the strong discords in the original version, and had rejected it on the grounds that it was 'not usual and therefore not right'. The weaker children, on the other hand, had failed to notice any difference between the two, and had merely guessed. These advanced idioms appeal especially to the highly experienced listener after a surfeit of the more usual harmony, but it appears that they are an unfair test for the inexperienced listener, for he may be penalized for noticing points that are passed over by the unmusical. When it is considered that Wagner had rather a bad reception from some of the expert critics of his day, it appears natural that the child should not appreciate this music. It was therefore thought better to omit such items, and also not to include any of the even more modern styles.

The reliability of the test was found by the split-half method. The removal of the score obtained in any individual item should reduce the reliability merely

---

[1] Even if some based their judgement on such an identification, it does not of necessity mean that the item is a bad one, for the power to detect this idiom is likely to be indicative of high capacity.

because it decreases the mark range. However, when the reliability was recalculated after the removal of each item in turn, in a few cases the coefficient actually improved, and it could therefore be assumed that the item concerned was not operating as intended. These items were played to groups of musical friends who were asked for their introspections. They indicated that the problem set was too difficult, with the result that the subjects merely guessed. To overcome this the contrast between the two versions of the item was made sharper.

A somewhat similar process was carried out with the whole test by correlating the entire battery with the teachers' ranking—and then correlating the total battery when the harmony test was removed. The latter should—and did—result in a fall of this coefficient, showing that the harmony test was contributing to the agreement between the two lists.

An approximate check was made on the effects of favourable opportunities, such as instrumental lessons or extra music at home, on the capacity to perform the tests. The method used is described more fully later and therefore need not be repeated here. It was concluded from the results that the test was not unduly influenced by such opportunities.

From time to time distribution curves were drawn, and adjustments were made in the difficulty of the items in order to get a suitable average mark and scatter. As the musical ages of the groups that were tested varied between the approximate limits of 6 and 26 years, this suggested an average age of about 16 years as being the best at which to get the most even distribution, and the relative difficulty of the items was accordingly adjusted.

With young children the curve is then skewed towards the lower end of the scale. This was especially marked in the test under discussion, because even when the pair of selections in each item was made as diverse as possible, while keeping within the sphere of what might be designated music, the two were still too close for very young children to make any distinction. This agrees with the findings of Belaiew-Exemplarsky (5) that young children did not appear to mind if the melody and accompaniment were in different keys.

When the test material had arrived at the stage at which alterations made very little difference to the marks, more attention was given to the technique of application. In the earliest testing the instructions were given verbally to the children, but they were later typed, and the examinees encouraged to ask questions. It appeared that their knowledge of technical terms, such as 'harmony', was negligible, and the word had to be replaced by 'notes underneath the tune'. As a result of these alterations the instructions became simple enough for a child aged 8 years to understand them easily. For later groups the children first read the instructions to themselves, and this was followed by a slow and deliberate reading by the supervisor after the children appeared to have finished reading. Questions were usually found to be unnecessary, and were certainly inadvisable in so far as they tended to make the procedure less standardized than was desirable. In the case of very young children who had difficulties with reading, the necessary explanations were added to make the meanings of all the words used quite clear.

Even then questions were very rare, and chiefly concerned with where their answers had to be filled in. In only 0·2 % of the papers was there any indication that the child had not understood the question properly. The most common mistake was that of filling in the answers in some place other than on the dotted lines provided, and, rather rarely, that of attempting to do some more advanced problem than that asked for, e.g. to name the notes in Test 1 instead of merely giving the number. Investigation into these cases showed that the majority were children of low I.Q. who would not normally be expected to be attending an ordinary school.

Another point that received attention was the timing of the items. The time allowed for decision was at first judged by the reaction of the children, and when they had finished writing their answer, the next item was proceeded with. Children were found to take about two to five seconds, but adults took longer and required up to about nine seconds. As the longer period gives the children a slight rest between the items, and it was desired to make the timing the same for all groups, that time (nine seconds) was adopted.

The pause between the two versions was adjusted by trial and error. If it were too short the children tended to confuse the two items, and if too long they were inclined to be distracted from the problem and to allow their attention to wander elsewhere. The best pause time appeared to be three seconds.

These times were found to be satisfactory, and for the harmony test and other appreciation tests, were kept constant throughout. With some of the ability tests, however, a longer decision period was found advisable for the earlier items, in order that the subject might become accustomed to the problem; it was also varied according to the nature of the task imposed.

When giving the tests through the medium of the piano it was very difficult to avoid occasional small slips or variations in playing. Further, the tests required constant practice if they were to be played in a satisfactory manner. In addition, the timing was very difficult unless there were two people present—one to play and the other to time the items.

It seemed necessary, before the work was carried out on any large scale, that an attempt should be made to remove these small divergences in timing and playing. Special gramophone records of the tests were therefore prepared in which the timing was done with a stop-watch by one person who announced the items, while a second played the tests. Any record on which there was a slip in the playing could then be discarded, and once a satisfactory record had been obtained, copies could be made as desired.

Recording brought with it some new problems, and the records had to pass through no less than four editions before a satisfactory set could be obtained. Thus some of the items had to be transposed a few notes higher or lower, as the extremely high notes sounded thin on the record, and the very low notes were sometimes a little unbalanced; also the order of difficulty was not quite the same. Two sets of records were prepared with the items in a different order so that if the tests were applied twice within a short period, there was little danger of the subjects being influenced by their previous answers.

These details of the methods of developing the harmony test apply, in most respects, to the other tests. As will be obvious, there were considerable changes introduced during the course of this work. This I regard as an important part of the investigation, for the improvement effected in the whole battery by this process of developing the separate tests may be gauged by the increase in the values of the correlation with the teachers' rankings, for they were 0·64, 0·78 and 0·82 at successive stages in the process.

Two other small points, concerned as much with the application of the whole set of tests as with the harmony test, may be mentioned. In the first place, it is extremely important to secure the co-operation of the subjects. If they are adults and feel that the tests have merit, this is quite easy. A large number were, however, children, and a definite attempt had to be made to put them at ease and to secure their maximum effort. In order to remove any examination atmosphere, which might have led them to an attempt at giving the answers expected rather than their own opinions, they were told that it was a musical competition and small prizes were given. The children actually were, with very few exceptions, much interested; especially the older ones, who broke into spontaneous discussions on the general method and on particular items when the testing was finished. There was also, frequently, a request for a repetition of the testing at a later date, and they were very anxious to know their scores. The latter were given to them privately if they came and asked, and very few of them failed to come.

In the second place, strict precautions were taken to prevent copying or whispering; indeed, any child who gave way to the temptation to talk was much frowned upon by his classmates. The teacher, who usually preferred to stay to hear the test, was provided with a seat at the back of the class, for a few of the more musical found it difficult not to give away their views on some of the items by their facial expressions, and the children were very ready to take their cue from this rather than to use their own powers. If the test ran into more than one school period, half-marked answer sheets were not returned to the children on the second occasion. Otherwise, they compared their scores while the marked papers were being given out, and those who had obtained high marks acquired a reputation which provided their neighbours with a great temptation to cheat. Even if they were prevented from copying by strict supervision, there remained the disadvantage that the weak child would be discouraged by the results on the first half of the paper and would tend to give up the attempt in the second half.

CHAPTER VII

THE SELECTION OF THE MOST EFFICIENT
AND SUITABLE TESTS

One aim of this work was to devise a series of tests which would estimate musical ability and appreciation within a reasonable examination time. This was considered to be one of about 80 minutes, for this is probably as long a time as may be taken at a stretch in music without undue fatigue. When all the tests were applied, they took two periods a week for nearly a term, and it was therefore necessary to eliminate a number. Those which were removed came under one or more of the following headings, being those which:

(a) Proved unworkable;

(b) Gave too much weight to acquired musical technicalities;

(c) Were inefficient as shown by correlations, etc.

(d) Took too much time in their application;

(e) Were limited in their range of difficulty (usually too easy for general application to a wide range of ages);

(f) Were redundant;

(g) Were difficult to apply in that they needed preliminary illustration;

(h) Could not be applied twice without considerable loss in efficiency.

(a) Tests which proved unworkable.

Test No. 16, in which the person is given a list of familiar tunes and asked to rank them in order of merit, proved unworkable after fairly extended trials, owing to the difficulty of finding ten tunes which were sufficiently familiar to most children. The original list was kindly provided by Burt,[1] and was submitted to several groups in one school. In spite of the fact that they were tunes which might reasonably be expected to be known by most people, it was found that there were several with which the children were entirely unacquainted, being songs which were not taught in that particular school. They were children from middle- or working-class districts and would not hear such songs at home. The list was revised so that it contained songs known to children of that school, and it was then submitted to a number of highly trained musicians in order to obtain an expert ranking. The results obtained by a fresh application of the test at this particular school indicated that the test was not without possibilities. When, however, the list was given at other schools, the number of melodies known was often only two or three; even when it was extended to twenty, and the children were asked to take any ten and rank them, the position was very little improved.[2] In these schools,

---

[1] This list was originally drawn up for another purpose, namely, to investigate types in listeners.

[2] If the tunes were played, in order to refresh their memory or to give them some acquaintance with unfamiliar tunes, the whole basis of the test was altered; it then became so similar to Test No. 15 that its inclusion in the series would be redundant.

consultations with the teachers showed that the melodies which received the most votes were those with which the children were familiar; the results were thus more dependent on the songs that they happened to have been taught than on the appreciative powers of the children. Really popular songs (dance tunes) were known to the majority of children, but such a list would be out of date in a few months and useless in any battery which was to be of permanent value.[1]

Adults who had some interest in music had no difficulties with the original list, and the test would therefore appear to be suitable for grading those who were already known to be interested in music. This is apparently the purpose for which Vernon intends his test on a choice of programme to be used.

The disturbing effects of familiarity mentioned for Test No. 16 were also apparent in the other test on melodic shape, No. 15, in which the subject was asked to choose the better of two played tunes. In this case, any tune that was known was nearly always chosen if it were compared with an unknown one, whatever the respective musical merits of the two. Some slight acquaintance with the weaker tunes and practically none with the better ones was a great handicap in performing the test, and this represented the position of most of the children. The subject is more fortunate if both are unknown, as he is then in a better position to regard them both in an unbiased fashion. Considerable familiarity with both tunes is a great advantage, as increasing acquaintance with a classical melody brings greater and greater appreciation, but with a weaker tune it brings boredom. It was also very difficult for the children to adopt an attitude of critical consideration unbiased by the emotions aroused by the conditions under which the melody had first been heard; thus a bad tune which had been learnt at a camp fire would probably always be preferred to a good one learnt in a singing lesson.

In spite of these disadvantages, the test proved more satisfactory than a repetition of Mohler's original experiment. The latter gave no scatter or average mark beyond those that would be expected by chance, whereas Test No. 15 did give some separation of the good children from the weaker ones; but it was not sufficient for the present purpose.

The general opinion was formed that Test No. 15 would be more suitable for musical adults than for general application. The test gave its two highest correlations with those on rhythm and phrasing, both of which also require for their successful performance an appreciation of melodic shape. It was decided that these two would involve the melodic aspect of music sufficiently to make it safe to omit the test on choice of tunes.

(b) *Tests which gave too much weight to acquired knowledge of musical technicalities.*

Whenever a group was tested at a new school the opinions of the music teacher were sought. Any criticisms were particularly directed against tests that involved acquired musical knowledge, on the grounds of the unequal opportunities that

[1] When an attempt was made to get an expert's ranking of popular songs, musicians did not know them, and, when they were shown the music, refused to consider them, declaring that they could not be included in any series of tests which claimed to be musical.

prevail in music. Many adults who were examined also objected to such tests because they had lost their familiarity with musical technicalities.

Tests which were found to be particularly subject to the effect of opportunity were:

No. 20. Questions on the symbols, etc. used in music.

No. 21. The recognition of tunes.

No. 22. The writing out of *God Save the King*.

No. 23. The writing from dictation of unknown tunes.

The scores of the first two of these gave little agreement with those obtained on the total battery. The tests were therefore probably inefficient, and were abandoned. The last two gave results which were in agreement with the general estimate, but they also correlated highly with the test on the comparison of a played tune with the notation, No. 12, and the latter was consequently taken as a substitute. Besides involving a smaller degree of familiarity with notation, No. 12 may be quickly and mechanically marked by the mere checking of the numbers against those written out on special marking cards. The other two tests, Nos. 22, 23, present special difficulties of marking in those cases in which the listener has made a mistake in the first note of a section, and has transposed the remainder, since it is hard to estimate the relative merit of such an answer against that of the subject who makes several mistakes, especially where such mistakes indicate little grasp of the general tune shape. An experienced music teacher might be able to settle the point to his own satisfaction, but another teacher would be likely to disagree, and any departure from mechanical marking must be regarded as undesirable in psychological tests.

(c) *Tests which were inefficient as shown by correlations, etc.*

From some of the early results, complete inter-correlations were calculated. These were a great aid in the elimination of the less satisfactory tests. In general, a test was considered satisfactory if its marks gave a reasonable correlation with the total for the whole battery, for it may then be reasonably assumed that it is assessing some musical capacity.[1] It was, however, not desirable that it should correlate too highly with other tests, for in that case it would be adding little to the information received.

Regard was had, too, for considerations other than statistical; for example, in a choice between two tests of a similar type, it was sometimes preferable to choose the one that was rather less efficient, from the point of view of the correlation, if the other involved a considerable number of musical technicalities. Again, a test might be aimed at assessing an ability considered desirable on general musical grounds (e.g. memory for 'time-patterns'), and yet might not correlate very well with the total battery because it is dealing with some capacity which is more or less independent of the general factor.

The test on stating the names of intervals, No. 13, gave a high correlation with

[1] It has been advanced in criticism that this means that the tests are selected so that they will demonstrate a general factor. However, the point mentioned was used as a guide, not as a rigid principle. My own attitude was that I had already shown that a general factor existed in a wide variety of tests, and that the process tended to eliminate some tests which contained little of the general factor, and were therefore unlikely to assess musical ability efficiently.

the total scores, but that on comparing intervals, No. 18, which was designed as an easier variant of the same aspect, showed very little agreement. This of itself indicates that the later test is probably unsatisfactory, and confirmation of this was obtained from an item analysis, the introspection of some of the subjects, and a comparison of the scores of the most musical quartile with those of the least musical one. The information obtained from the last consideration is contained, in a general way, in the correlation coefficient obtained between the test and the total battery (which is assumed to be estimating musical capacity); but the further process adds details and allows more cases to be easily considered—380 were actually used. In only four of the items did the group get an average score which was higher than the chance total, i.e. the problem was probably a very difficult one and the majority of the subjects were merely guessing. This would not be of great importance if the test, though difficult, were efficient in picking out the more musical children, but an analysis of the answers of the upper quartile (their ability being judged on the results of the total battery) showed that their scores were low. Either the problem was too difficult for them (although some were musical adolescents of 18 years), or there were reasons which caused the musical subjects to give the wrong or chance answers for some items.

The introspections of various people who were known to be musical, were obtained. They were asked to examine carefully their method of performing the test, and especially to reconsider in detail those cases in which they had given the wrong answer at the first attempt.[1] The results of their introspections may be illustrated by one, apparently very easy, item in which two octaves were played at an interval of a seventh apart. This was sometimes designated 'different' by expert musicians who could accomplish the other test on intervals with ease. Referring to this item, one musician stated: 'I heard the first interval and labelled it an octave; the second was played and my immediate reaction was "seventh" and so I wrote down "different".' Thus the musician was in danger of confusing the interval between the two chords with the interval contained in the second pair of notes; it is, indeed, the second interval relationship that is presented to the examinee. The latter is, therefore, following in some degree the instruction to compare the first interval he hears with the second. Similarly another, in explanation of his mistake, stated: 'The intervals are listened to in a way that I would adopt for any harmonic progression—the second is listened to in relation to the first; the two are not heard in isolation, and then compared.' When the subject was told to analyse the first interval, and then the second, and finally to write down whether the two were the same or different, the musician was undoubtedly superior to the unmusical person in this task.[2] However, this is a departure from the normal habits

[1] It may be mentioned that this had already been done to a limited extent with all the tests before they had been applied to any large group. In spite of the adverse opinions obtained on this particular test, it was nevertheless applied to the large number of subjects mentioned above in order to get more certain experimental evidence.

[2] Had the instructions been so altered as to cast the problem in this new form, the task set would be identical with the other interval test, except that it would have been a more difficult, rather than the easier, version intended.

of the musician in listening to music. Obviously, any test which penalizes the subject who follows good habits of listening to music must be discarded.

The test suffers from the same disadvantage as that found by Heinlein (54) in the case of the Seashore consonance test, namely, the difficulty that the musical subject has in considering two successive chords in isolation from each other. The Seashore test also had to be abandoned by its compiler.

(d) Tests which took too much time in their application.

A test which takes a very long time to apply is not worth its place in the battery if it thereby excludes the use of two or three other tests of greater combined efficiency. Test No. 17, on pace of performance, was of this type, for the repetition of twenty items, each of which was played at three different speeds, took 40 minutes to give—this was about two-thirds of the time in which it was hoped to give the whole of the final series. A further disadvantage of this test was that many persons—especially the more musical ones—found it extremely fatiguing, for they had to readjust themselves to sixty changes of time within a limited period. So marked was this that a large proportion of the examinees stated that they were too tired to follow it by another test, if they were to do justice to the latter. The test on pace of performance was, therefore, discarded with regret.

(e) Tests which were too limited in range of difficulty.

It was decided to include in the final battery tests of such a range that they could be used on very young children and on musical adults. This has the advantage of economy of labour in standardizing only one set, and also of enabling a true perspective of the musical capacity of examinees of widely different ages to be obtained. Certain of the earlier tests were found to be too limited for this purpose because the capacity investigated seemed to be fairly fully developed by 11 years of age;[1] this meant that for older persons there was very little scatter in the scores, as the majority of the subjects obtained nearly full marks. Such a test was that of giving the best descriptive title to a played piece of music (No. 14). The test as I used it proved too easy for those over 12 years of age. If the titles had been further refined, or a more difficult choice of words presented, then the problem would have developed into one of the appreciation of subtle distinctions in words expressing emotions, as the opinion of most musicians is that programmatic music can only legitimately be applied to emotions, and not to concrete things or events. The addition of a list of the meanings of such terms as 'anxiety', 'worry' or 'repentance' would not meet the case, as it could not convey to young children the feeling of emotional states to which they were strangers and which they were being asked to compare with those aroused by the music.

---

[1] I hope to develop some of these tests at a future date, in connection with a subsidiary battery to be used for grading children below 10 years of age on a wider scale than is possible with the present series which are intended for general application.

(f) *Tests which were redundant.*

The intercorrelation showed that some of the tests were assessing very similar capacities. Two such tests were 'time-pattern dictation' and 'rhythm', a result which would be expected on musical grounds, as the former is a subsidiary aspect of the latter. The first involves some acquired notation, a particular disadvantage in this case, as the amount of practice given in writing down such time-patterns varies considerably from school to school. With the rhythm test, however, the tasks set can be made extremely difficult without needing, or being noticeably influenced by, any acquired knowledge of musical technicalities. Secondly, it is closer to the appreciation required in listening to normal music. Finally, it can be applied repeatedly to the same people without deterioration in efficiency in a way that the other test could not. The rhythm test was therefore preferred.

Test No. 5, dealing with taste in the harmonization of a melody, and No. 25 on chord progressions, were set as alternatives, and their high correlation supports this procedure. The former is the more musical and interesting, and so is the more successful in securing the co-operation of musical examinees. Moreover, it can be set with a wider distribution of difficulty among the items because the problems involve many more points of distinction. All this results in a much better distribution of the scores. Consequently Test No. 25 was omitted.

Another case of high correlation was that shown between Test No. 19, on stating which part is moving when two chords are played, and No. 2, on stating the direction of movement of a note. As the former test used three parts, and as in the other the choice was up, down, or the same, the chance score in each was identical. The latter could, however, be taken to a much greater stage of difficulty by increasing the number of notes in the chord. If the first be made more difficult by a similar addition of notes, the subject who is unversed in musical technicalities has great difficulty in describing what he has heard. The second test can also be given much more rapidly, and, as it was desired to have one test which called for speed of decision, this was an added argument in its favour, and so Test No. 2 was adopted.

A fourth case of high correlation occurred with the three tests which dealt with chord analysis. They were No. 1, on stating the number of notes in a chord; No. 13, on naming intervals; and No. 11, on stating whether a note is in the chord which follows. Of these, the first was preferred as it could be arranged to give a wider range of difficulty than the other two; it had a very low chance score compared with the third, and less acquired knowledge than the second. It was not known whether it would prove to be as successful when recorded as it was on the piano, since, even with the extremely expensive apparatus that is used by the B.B.C. and the gramophone companies, there is always some quavering in pitch and unevenness in recording the notes of a chord. All three were therefore recorded on gramophone disks for further trials before making the final decision.

Of the other types of tests mentioned as having been inefficient, two remain. First, tests needing preliminary illustration, an example of which was the test on key change; secondly, tests which could not be applied to the same group twice without loss in efficiency, of which examples were the test on the recognition of tunes, and the test on the most suitable title. These tests have already been discussed in detail and need not be dealt with any further.

This selection had left thirteen tests, and although it was realized that there were more than were actually required, for they took two hours to give, they were all made into gramophone records, and applied to a group of 138 children, aged 12–16 years, for further trials. On the results of these it was decided to remove six more tests in order to obtain a series with a playing time of about 50 minutes.

In the first place No. 1, as stated above, was preferred to the other two on chord analysis, provided that the notes could be clearly heard when they had been made into gramophone records. The test was now rather more difficult, but people who were known to be highly musical could get all, or practically all, the items right without difficulty (this included a boy aged 15 years, with a score of 19 out of 20) so that it was assumed that the recording was clear enough for testing purposes.

Both Test No. 8, on Cadences, and Test No. 9, on Discords, proved too easy to give a symmetrical scatter. Not only does this make the interpretation and comparison of correlation coefficients somewhat dubious, but it also means that the test has very little separating value when used on adults. These tests, moreover, are likely, in the light of such researches as those of Bugg[14] and Gardner & Pickford[42], to be dealing with acquired habits. Although the speedy learning of such a habit might reasonably be supposed to indicate some form of musical capacity, the child who has heard very little music would probably be at a distinct disadvantage.[1] The tests correlated well with that on harmony—as indeed might be expected on musical grounds, for both discords and cadences are quite conspicuously involved in harmonic structure, so that it was considered safe to omit these two tests if that on harmony were retained. There are possibilities of their future development for use with very young children for whom the harmony test is too difficult.

The test on key change, No. 10, gave results which showed a satisfactory scatter and which indicated that it had promise of being a good diagnostic test. However, it appeared essential to give a short introductory lesson which included practice with suitable examples, before applying the test, in order to make clear to the listeners exactly what was required of them. This considerably lessened its value as a psychological test, and it was therefore rejected.

Of the eight remaining tests only one, No. 12, on the comparison of the notation with a played tune, was likely to be at all influenced by acquired musical knowledge. It had been left in after the first selection as it was representative of a large number of tests of that type which are widely used in school work and have also been fairly frequently applied by psychologists. The familiarity with musical technicalities required is not large, being limited to the amount of tonic sol-fa notation likely to be taught to most children up to the age of 10 years. The test was successful when

---

[1] It is difficult to trace extreme lack of opportunity to hear music at home, school or from the radio, but comparatively easy to find out those who have had facilities above the normal, so that this point could not be investigated.

applied to children between the ages of 12 and 15 years, and to musical adults; but with average adults there were frequent complaints about the handicap involved in performing a test which contained notation with which they were no longer familiar. Some of the young children also found it difficult for the same reason and therefore this test was rejected.

If musical capacity were to consist of a number of isolated factors, then the procedure of reducing the tests from twenty-four to the comparatively small number of seven might be open to criticism on the ground that tests for certain of these factors had been removed in deriving the short battery. However, very high correlations have been obtained between the original twenty-four tests, the thirteen intermediate ones, and the final seven. These are given in a later chapter. Even if the theory of isolated factors be correct, it may therefore be concluded that no vital test is missing from the short series.

My own opinion is that although musical capacity may be complex, there is nevertheless a strong general factor (designated μ) underlying ability to perform a wide variety of musical tests. Evidence on this point has been advanced elsewhere [168]. If this be accepted, then the reduction to a smaller number of tests is not open to objection.

Details of the extent to which the above process resulted in a series of tests which would satisfy the criteria laid down are given in the next chapter. Owing to lack of space the music of the tests used cannot be given in this publication but may be found in my thesis [169], together with details of the instructions used for all twenty-six tests. A copy of the instructions for the short series is, however, given below.

STANDARDIZED TESTS OF MUSICAL INTELLIGENCE

Test 1. Chord Analysis. (Detecting the number of notes played in a single chord)

Either a single note or a chord (group of notes struck together) will be played. Mark with an **X** the number of notes that is played. Use the numbers provided below for your answers. The number of the question will be announced by the loud speaker.

If in doubt about your answer in any of the tests, **do not leave blank, but GUESS.**

Practice:

A B C D

1	1	**X**	1
X	2	2	2
3	**X**	3	3
4	4	4	**X**
5	5	5	5
6	6	6	6

Answers:

1	2	3	4	5	6	7	8	9	10
1	1	1	1	1	1	1	1	1	1
2	2	2	2	2	2	2	2	2	2
3	3	3	3	3	3	3	3	3	3
4	4	4	4	4	4	4	4	4	4
5	5	5	5	5	5	5	5	5	5
6	6	6	6	6	6	6	6	6	6

11	12	13	14	15	16	17	18	19	20
1	1	1	1	1	1	1	1	1	1
2	2	2	2	2	2	2	2	2	2
3	3	3	3	3	3	3	3	3	3
4	4	4	4	4	4	4	4	4	4
5	5	5	5	5	5	5	5	5	5
6	6	6	6	6	6	6	6	6	6

Test 2. Pitch Change. (Detecting an alteration of a single note in a repeated chord)

Two chords are played. Sometimes one note, not more, is altered in the second chord. If the two chords are the same, mark 'S' in the place provided for your answer. If there is a difference, state whether the altered note moves up or down. Marking 'U' for up, and 'D' for down. If in doubt, then guess.

Practice:

A B C

U	U	**X**
D	**X**	D
X	S	S

Answers:

1	2	3	4	5	6	7	8	9	10	11	12	13	14	15
U	U	U	U	U	U	U	U	U	U	U	U	U	U	U
D	D	D	D	D	D	D	D	D	D	D	D	D	D	D
S	S	S	S	S	S	S	S	S	S	S	S	S	S	S

16	17	18	19	20	21	22	23	24	25	26	27	28	29	30
U	U	U	U	U	U	U	U	U	U	U	U	U	U	U
D	D	D	D	D	D	D	D	D	D	D	D	D	D	D
S	S	S	S	S	S	S	S	S	S	S	S	S	S	S

Test 3. Memory. (Detecting an alteration of note in a short melody)

A tune is played twice. On the second playing one note, not more, may be altered. The first four tunes are of three notes, the next four tunes have four notes, and so on, getting longer towards the end. The number of notes is shown by the number of dots in the answer places. See whether you can say which note is altered. The altered note may be shown by marking through the dot which is written for the note in the answer place. Suppose, for example, that the second note of No. 5 is altered it would be shown like this No. 5 ● ♦ ● ● or if it were the fourth note, like this No. 5 ● ● ● ♦
        1 2 3 4   1 2 3 4

If the two tunes are the same write S; if they appear different but you do not know which one is altered, do not leave a blank but guess.

Practice: A ● ● ♦   B ● ♦ ●   C ● ● ● ● ♦ ●
                    1 2 3   1 2 3   1 2 3 4 5 6

Answers:

3-note tunes.

1 ● ● ●   2 ● ● ●   3 ● ● ●   4 ● ● ●
   1 2 3   1 2 3   1 2 3   1 2 3

4-note tunes

5 ● ● ● ●   6 ● ● ● ●   7 ● ● ● ●   8 ● ● ● ●
   1 2 3 4   1 2 3 4   1 2 3 4   1 2 3 4

5-note tunes

9 ● ● ● ● ●   10 ● ● ● ● ●   11 ● ● ● ● ●   12 ● ● ● ● ●
   1 2 3 4 5   1 2 3 4 5   1 2 3 4 5   1 2 3 4 5

6-note tunes

13 ● ● ● ● ● ●   14 ● ● ● ● ● ●   15 ● ● ● ● ● ●
    1 2 3 4 5 6   1 2 3 4 5 6   1 2 3 4 5 6

7-note tunes

16 ● ● ● ● ● ●   17 ● ● ● ● ● ● ●   18 ● ● ● ● ● ● ●
    1 2 3 4 5 6   1 2 3 4 5 6 7   1 2 3 4 5 6 7

8-note tunes

19 ● ● ● ● ● ● ●   20 ● ● ● ● ● ● ●   21 ● ● ● ● ● ● ● ●
    1 2 3 4 5 6 7   1 2 3 4 5 6 7   1 2 3 4 5 6 7 8

22 ● ● ● ● ● ● ● ●   23 ● ● ● ● ● ● ● ●   24 ● ● ● ● ● ● ● ●
    1 2 3 4 5 6 7 8   1 2 3 4 5 6 7 8   1 2 3 4 5 6 7 8

9-note tunes

25 ● ● ● ● ● ● ● ● ●   26 ● ● ● ● ● ● ● ● ●   27 ● ● ● ● ● ● ● ● ●
    1 2 3 4 5 6 7 8 9   1 2 3 4 5 6 7 8 9   1 2 3 4 5 6 7 8 9

10-note tunes

28 ● ● ● ● ● ● ● ● ● ●   29 ● ● ● ● ● ● ● ● ● ●   30 ● ● ● ● ● ● ● ● ● ●
    1 2 3 4 5 6 7 8 9 10   1 2 3 4 5 6 7 8 9 10   1 2 3 4 5 6 7 8 9 10

Test 4. Rhythmic accent. (*Choosing the better rhythmic accent in two performances*)

The same tune will be played twice. Sometimes the accentuated (more strongly played) notes are in a different place the second time. If the two playings are the same mark 'S'. If they are different, choose the style of playing which you think better fits the tune. Mark 'A' for the first and 'B' for the second. If you notice a difference but cannot make up your mind which you prefer, then guess.

Answers: 1   2   3   4   5   6   7   8   9   10   11   12   13   14

A	A	A	A	A	A	A	A	A	A	A	A	A	A
B	B	B	B	B	B	B	B	B	B	B	B	B	B
S	S	S	S	S	S	S	S	S	S	S	S	S	S

Test 5. Harmony. (*Judging the more appropriate of two harmonizations*)

The same tune will be played twice. Sometimes the second playing has different notes below the tune (the notes played by the left hand may be different). If they are the same, mark 'S'. If they are different, mark which you think the better, 'A' or 'B'. If in doubt, then guess.

Answers: 1   2   3   4   5   6   7   8   9   10   11   12   13   14

A	A	A	A	A	A	A	A	A	A	A	A	A	A
B	B	B	B	B	B	B	B	B	B	B	B	B	B
S	S	S	S	S	S	S	S	S	S	S	S	S	S

Test 6. Intensity. (*Judging the more appropriate mode of varying loudness—crescendo, decrescendo, etc.—in two performances of the same melody*)

The same tune will be played to you twice. Sometimes the louder and quieter portions are in different places when the tune is played the second time. If they are the same, mark 'S'. If they are different, choose the style of playing which better fits the tune, 'A' or 'B'. If in doubt, then guess.

Answers: 1   2   3   4   5   6   7   8   9   10   11   12   13   14

A	A	A	A	A	A	A	A	A	A	A	A	A	A
B	B	B	B	B	B	B	B	B	B	B	B	B	B
S	S	S	S	S	S	S	S	S	S	S	S	S	S

Test 7. Phrasing. (*Judging the more appropriate phrasing—grouping of notes by pauses, legato and staccato playing, etc.—in two performances*)

The same piece of music is played twice. Sometimes the second playing has the notes differently grouped (different groups of notes may be played with short sharp strokes, or so that they follow on smoothly, etc.). The general effect may be compared to punctuation—that is, the use of commas, etc., in ordinary writing. If the two playings are the same, mark 'S'. If they are different choose the style of playing which you think better fits the music. If in doubt, then guess.

Answers: 1   2   3   4   5   6   7   8   9   10   11   12   13   14

A	A	A	A	A	A	A	A	A	A	A	A	A	A
B	B	B	B	B	B	B	B	B	B	B	B	B	B
S	S	S	S	S	S	S	S	S	S	S	S	S	S

CHAPTER VIII

THE SATISFACTION OF THE ADOPTED CRITERIA BY THE SHORT SERIES OF TESTS

Certain criteria have been laid down which it was thought desirable for any series of psychological tests of musical capacity to satisfy; it will now be considered how far the short series, which was selected with these conditions in mind, has actually satisfied them. They will be taken in the order previously given, which was based more on convenience of discussion than on relative importance.

1. *They should be acceptable in their basic principles to musicians.*

It is essential to gain the co-operation of those who are likely to use any series of tests, and these will include not only psychologists, but also educationists in general and music teachers in particular. These last are usually highly trained— more as specialists in their own subject than as teachers—and are very sensitive to the musical value and basis of any tests that are advanced. They are therefore unlikely to use those containing unmusical material. Throughout the previous work this point had been kept well in mind, and constant touch had been maintained with other musicians and teachers of music, in order both to make use of their criticisms and experience, and to make sure that the music used was acceptable to them as true art.

Furthermore, if the person tested were highly musical, it appeared desirable that he himself should be convinced of the close relation between the problems he was asked to do, and music as he actually knew it. His interests lay in the direction of music, and the tests were likely to be more effective if they tapped this interest. It was clearly shown by the introspections of those subjects who were known to be musical, and had shown up very badly in the Seashore tests, that part of their failure was due to lack of co-operative interest, for they became a little irritated with those of the tests that claimed to be dealing with music but proved, in fact, to be concerned with taps and buzzer noises. It was noticeable that the listeners were more stimulated and did relatively better on the memory and rhythm tests than on the others, and this was probably because their connection with music was more apparent.

Seashore (136) has himself emphasized the importance of this matter, and has quoted cases of well-known musicians who have done badly in his tests. It is true that he found that, after some conversation in which he was able to demonstrate his theories, the performance on a second testing was considerably improved; but it is to be remembered that had these people been unknown subjects, tested by normal procedure, they would have been missed in any search for those with musical talent. Therefore, even if the capacity could be estimated by the use of non-musical material (and this has yet to be proved), there are distinct advantages in the use of musical tests as here employed.

The guiding principle in compiling the appreciation tests was to use really good compositions by able composers whose authority could pass unchallenged, so that the material used would be truly musical. Preliminary experiments, in which the effect of using known tunes in the harmony test had been investigated, tended to show that these items were no easier than those which were unknown. When the tests were more developed the point was further investigated, using larger numbers of examinees, who were asked to underline their answers in those cases in which the music was familiar. Among the younger children, the number of known items was exceedingly small; e.g. in one group of 36 boys, aged 13 years, only 1·15 % of the items were stated to be familiar. The use of known items can have had no significant effect on these scores, and their papers were not further analysed, but attention was directed towards the older groups. In 100 cases (boys aged 16–18 years) taken from schools in which there was a considerable amount of musical activity, 11·17 % of the music was known; the highest was 45 pieces, and the lowest was 3. The distribution curve is given below. From a rough survey of the answers

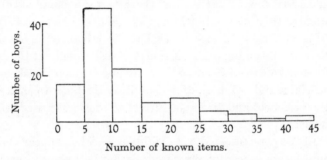

Fig. 1. The distribution of the known items in 100 boys.

it seemed that the number known was a fairly good indication of opportunity and interest, but did not show any marked connection with ability as estimated by the total score. In individual cases where the number of familiar pieces was sufficiently high to give significant figures, calculation showed that the percentages of correct answers in the known and the unknown music were almost the same. A large number of papers was thus examined, and of the total 8000 answers, the number correct was 4191, or 52·40 %. Of these there were 1171 known pieces, and here the number correct was 614, or 52·43 %. These figures are in remarkable agreement, and demonstrate that the results are but little, if at all, affected by the use of music that is familiar.

This was not altogether unexpected, for the fundamental discrimination in the mode of playing must still be made, whether the music is familiar or not. The problem to be faced in actual music is also of this character, namely an appreciation of the performance of music, some of which may be known.[1]

[1] The possibility has been advanced in friendly criticism that familiarity might be an aid to some and a hindrance to others (by prejudicing them in favour of any new performance, no matter how bad). It is not thought that this is likely in the music used in the present tests—nor, if it were true, would it be expected that the two effects would exactly cancel out, as must also be supposed on the figures given.

2. *They should not be unduly influenced by training or opportunity.*

Opportunities in music may be simply those of hearing more than the average amount of good music, or they may extend to definite training in singing or on an instrument.

With regard to the former, the results given in the preceding section tend to show that the marks are not unduly influenced by an acquaintance with the music used in the tests, and this may be taken as a sampling of the acquaintance with music in general. Also, evidence will be later advanced (in dealing with the effect of environment) to show that opportunity to hear music at home does not appear to affect the scores appreciably. It may be assumed, therefore, that the tests are not greatly affected by opportunities somewhat above the normal to hear good music. It might still be the case, of course, that exceptional opportunities in this respect would affect the results.

With regard to the effect of training on an instrument, the most marked would obviously occur in any tests which involved a knowledge of musical technicalities. However, every attempt has been made to avoid the latter, e.g. the only words that might be considered in this category were those of 'note', and the terms 'up' and 'down' as applied to music, both of which are well within the capacity of a child of 8 years. In order to obtain experimental evidence on whether or not the scores were affected by training on a musical instrument, 271 children, aged 12 years, were divided into three broad musical ability groups, as judged on their performance in the tests. The groups were the AB, or the above average, who represent the top 30 % of an average sample of the population; the C, or average, being the middle 40 %; and the DE, or below average who are the lowest 30 %.

The percentage of children in each group who were undergoing executive training was then calculated. It was found that no significant difference existed between the percentages of instrumentalists among the musically bright, the average or the musically dull. Had training of this kind greatly influenced the test results the performers would have been found mostly in the top group.

Table I. *Ability and Instrumental Training.*

Ability Group[1]	AB (above average) Top 38 %	C (average) Middle 40 %	DE (below average) Bottom 22 %
Percentage of each group who are studying some instrument	28 %	28 %	23 %

Further evidence is furnished by the fact that several groups who had been tested twice, with a period of from one to five years between the two assessments,

[1] In the actual group used, the percentages were a little on the above average side, as there was a larger proportion of High School children than would be present in a strictly average sample.

gave high correlations between the scores on the first and second occasions, in spite of the fact that many had been continuing their study of instruments during this period, a few had commenced, and others had given up, playing. The figures are considered in more detail later.

It was thought by musicians that the first three of these tests, being of a problem type, might be particularly liable to be affected by practice and training. If this were true, then it would be expected that when school music ceases—as it does for most boys at fourteen—there would be a considerable falling off in the ability to do these tests. However, when curves of the average marks for these tests were plotted, far from there being any falling off in ability, there was a steady and continuous growth at a rate which was approximately the same as when the boys were having music lessons.[1]

In order to gain a little further evidence on the influence of special teaching, some lessons on the material of the tests were given between two testings of the same group, but no marked improvement could be observed in the scores. For this, 50 boys, aged 15 and 16 years, were divided into two groups that were approximately equal in size, intelligence and musical opportunities. They were first tested in the normal manner, and the second testing was spread out so that one test only was performed in a school period. The control group had no lessons, but the other had a twenty-minute lesson; illustrated by examples played on the piano, on the material of a test, followed by a discussion which aroused a considerable amount of interest. They were then told that the test would be tried again in order to see what improvement they could make on their original score. The improvement of this group was 4·1 % and the correlation of the two scores was 0·93; the improvement of the control group was 3·4 %, and their correlation was 0·89. The improvement due to teaching was thus quite small.

3. *It is preferable that the battery should be comprehensive in its power to assess subjects of widely differing capacity.*

That extremely wide individual differences in musical capacity exist may be seen from the distribution curves given later. To separate such wide extremes there must be a corresponding range in the problems set. Actually the items have been so graded that the easiest examples can be performed by a child of 8 years, while the most difficult would tax the powers of an accomplished musician. Children below 8 years have not been tested on any considerable scale, as these are group tests, and younger children cannot read, write or understand the instructions easily enough. It is, however, quite possible to pick out children of marked ability by individual testing before 8 years of age. It is hoped to carry out further investigations into the problem of grading very young children by the use of specially designed tests. Some preliminary work that had been commenced in this direction was interrupted by the outbreak of war.

[1] Although the effect of this school training appears to be small, the effects of concentrated daily practice, such as that undertaken by a student at a music college, might possibly be more marked. An opportunity to investigate this point did not, however, occur.

A battery which is comprehensive in its power to assess subjects of widely differing capacity is not very efficient for testing young children, for a fairly large percentage of the questions are too advanced for them. This hardly arises at the other end of the scale, as with adolescents or adults there are still some of very low ability who can answer only a few questions. (The same difficulty has, of course, been found with the Seashore tests and with sets of general intelligence questions, such as those of Binet, which aim at assessing mental ages with a single collection of tests.) In the present series, the majority of the items of the last four tests were too difficult for most children of 9 years and under, who only scored a guessing total. It would appear to be rather a waste of time to apply these particular tests to such children unless they had proved, by their performance in Tests Nos. 1–3, that they were above average. If the children were graded on the results of the first three tests only, the smallness of the number of items on which the assessment was based considerably reduced the reliability; a method of improving the reliability which was used was to apply the first three tests twice, using the alternative form of memory test for the second examination, and then to take the average of the two scores. If it were desired to get an (approximate) value of the musical age, a guessing total was assumed for the remaining items of the battery (i.e. 27 marks), and this was added to the score for the first three. A few of the better children would then be tested with the whole battery.

A similar method has been followed with slightly older children of about 10 years, by applying the first three complete tests, and then the first ten (easier) items of the four appreciation tests. An assumed guessing total of 13 marks for the remaining items that were not attempted was added to the score thus obtained.

4. *They should cover a sufficiently wide sample of musical talents.*

As has already been pointed out, the width of the samples of musical talents which it is necessary to take in a battery of tests will largely depend on the existence or otherwise of a general factor underlying ability to perform a wide variety of musical tests. Many of the investigations carried out by previous workers were considered to be unsatisfactory because one, or only a few, aspects of musical ability were estimated and the results assumed to be diagnostic of general musical ability. It would be necessary to show, before a small number of tests was considered satisfactory, either that the general factor existed, or that those few tests gave a reasonable agreement with a much larger battery which included tests covering all the important aspects of musical capacity. It has already been shown that these conditions were satisfied in the case of the present tests.

5. *They should fulfil certain statistical criteria of reliability.*

The reliability of the series of thirteen tests was 0·95, found by two applications to the same group of 71 boys, aged 15 years. That of the short series of seven tests was 0·915 with a group of 41 boys, and 0·91 with another group of 65 boys of the same age. The reliabilities were all calculated by the product moment method.

The higher coefficient with the longer series is probably due to the larger number of items (there were 280 instead of 160). The reliability of the total of the first three tests was 0·89, and that of the last four 0·84, in each case with a group of 41. These reliabilities were found with a normal class of boys who had no particular interest in music, or in doing well in the test; they tended to lose interest in the second testing, which was taken a week after the first. With adults or musical people the reliabilities would probably be even higher.

The battery was thus found to have as high a reliability as could be expected of tests concerned with the aesthetics of music. Small changes in external conditions, such as a passing car or a howling wind, are more likely to affect music tests than those of other cognitive abilities, and school conditions are often far from ideal in this respect. Individuals react differently to these disturbing conditions, and also to a second testing, thus lowering the reliability.[1]

6. *They should be suitable for repeated applications to the same subjects without any great loss in efficiency.*

Some of the tests that were used in the preliminary series, or by past investigators, cannot be applied twice to the same person, as he is likely to remember sufficient of his previous answers for these to be of assistance at the second attempt. A test of this nature was that on titles, in which not only was the subject likely to have some assistance from a memory of his own answers, but also the answers were discussed among the members of the group when the testing was over. As no estimate of the development of musical ability can be made unless the same test is used throughout the investigation, this made such tests unsuited for the present purposes.

The tests might normally be expected to be used not more frequently than at two-yearly intervals. In the case of the present series when groups were re-tested after a lapse of a year or more, no advantage due to the previous testing could be detected, for the improvement was not more than would be normally expected after a year's development. For the purposes of calculating reliability, some groups were tested twice within a week, and there was then a small improvement in the score of about 4 %. This was found to be due almost entirely to the memory test (No. 3).[2] To meet the rather rare circumstances of testing after a very short

---

[1] As an interesting sidelight on this point the personal reliabilities were calculated for a number of the boys, i.e. the persons were correlated instead of the tests. The marks obtained by an individual were expressed as deviations about his own average for each assessment, and the two were correlated. It was found that this self-reliability threw some interesting light on the temperament of the individual. The characters of the boys were fairly well known (I had taken them all for a year, and many of them for several years) and the figures obtained agreed in general with the estimate formed by general impression in subjects other than music. Thus a steady hard-working boy achieved 0·93, and a rather slap-dash youth, who was subject to considerable variations in temperamental outlook, had a coefficient of only 0·5. The majority were in the region of 0·8. Individual day to day variations are extremely likely to influence the reliability of aesthetic tests, for the latter are influenced by affective as well as cognitive factors.

[2] Even Seashore's 'nonsense' memory test is subject to the same disadvantage.

interval a second version of that test was compiled, using different items but of the same order of difficulty. No increase in score was noticeable for the other tests; it was not expected, for it has previously been shown that a familiarity with the music of the tests does not affect the results, and whether this acquaintance had come from normal experience or from a previous testing would not be expected to be of material importance.

7. *They should give a score which is easily evaluated on a standardized scale.*

The results of testing an individual are of little value unless the psychologist can convert them into some figure which has a meaning apart from the actual material used. There are exceedingly few musical tests which have been so standardized, and as far as work in this country is concerned, the only battery commonly used is that of Seashore. He expressly warns those using his tests against any system of averaging the marks or the ranking obtained from each test, but recommends the structure of a musical profile, which must then be interpreted. The latter is a difficult task unless the supervisor can obtain adequate information of the relative importance of the basic abilities that are therein tested.

There seems no objection in the present series to a simple addition of the scores of each test; the totals can be quickly and easily converted into a musical age by the use of a graph or the simple formula $\dfrac{\text{Mark} - 23}{3 \cdot 1}$, and then into a musical quotient, or, if preferred, into a musical grade according to the procedure mentioned in a later chapter. In order to obtain the maximum efficiency in measuring general musical capacity, the marks should, strictly speaking, be weighted. However, the ordinary totals give a very close approximation to the correctly weighted total, so that for all practical purposes the weighting is unnecessary. If it is desired to gain some information with regard to the person's comparative efficiency in the various sections, then his mark may be compared with that of the general level for his age, as shown in the curve for the individual tests which are given elsewhere (169).

8. *They should be economical in the time required for their application.*

An hour is usually regarded as a satisfactory time for a psychological test. The present series occupies nine 10-inch records, which means an actual playing time of about 50 minutes, so that with a group of older subjects the test takes an hour, although younger children need a little longer, as they are rather slow in reading the instructions.

This testing time may be split without appreciably affecting the resultant scores, no significant difference being noted when a group was tested twice with both playings running straight through, and a second group was tested twice, but with the second testing taken in short sections. From this it may also be assumed that the fatigue effects are small. There is an appreciable rest period after each item, and between the separate tests, and no single test lasts for more than 12 minutes. Also, tests with harmony alternate with those that are melodic, in order to reduce the likelihood of boredom.

9. *They should correlate well with an exterior criterion.*

Mursell states that 'validity coefficients (for music tests) are conspicuous by their absence' (107). This is probably because it is extremely hard to secure a ranking of a school group from a music teacher, who usually has a large number of pupils through his hands in a week; often with classes twice the normal size. Consequently the teachers do not get to know their pupils individually, and although they can usually pick out the five or six best, this is of little use for calculating a validity coefficient, especially as such opinions are based chiefly on singing ability, which may, or may not, be indicative of general musical capacity.

The only available correlations would seem to be those with the Seashore battery, or for the Seashore battery taken with other aspects which are often not strictly testing—such as that of Lamp & Keys (84) which includes length of finger, and intelligence tests. The values that have been obtained with the Seashore tests are extremely low, and the figures obtained by two investigators who have carried out the process for the complete tests are as follows:

Table II. *Validity of the Seashore Tests.*

	Pitch	Intensity	Time	Consonance	Rhythm	Tonal memory	Average
Brown (13)	0·15	0·11	0·15	0·17	0·17	0·41	0·35
Mursell (106)	0·11	0·07	0·20	− 0·27	0·25	0·19	0·08

The probable errors of Brown's correlations are all of the order of 0·06, and those of Mursell, 0·08. Brown obtains a low validity coefficient for the average of the whole tests, and that of Mursell is seen to be negligible.

The writer has made a habit of asking the teacher of each group tested if he could supply a ranking, but out of several hundred groups thus tested, only three could be obtained.[1] The correlations of the test ranking with these were 0·64, 0·78 and 0·82. The first was obtained from a German group of 45 girls, and the teacher had marks under the headings of singing, aural work and theory. The tests used were the early piano ones. The difference in the two rankings was mainly accounted for by a comparatively few pupils who were placed low by the teacher and considerably higher by the tests. Discussion with the teacher revealed the fact that these girls could not sing, and the difference in the two estimates could partly be explained by the weighting that singing would have in the teacher's estimate. In the second case a small mixed group of fifteen could be reliably assessed by the teacher, for they were all piano pupils. His ranking was based on performing ability taken in conjunction with the speed of learning. The tests were the earliest of the recorded versions. In the last group the writer was able to assess the boys on their performance on orchestral instruments, again taking into account the time they had

---

[1] Further validity coefficients of 0·90 and 0·77 based on the ranking of six and nineteen adults respectively, who were pupils of training college lecturers, have since been obtained.

been studying.[1] This group consisted of 34 boys, and their ages varied from 12 to 18 years. After ranking they were tested, their scores converted to musical quotients, and the new ranking thus obtained was correlated with the first.

Having regard to the difficulties of securing validity coefficients, and to the low figures obtained by other workers, the results obtained in this respect with the later versions of the tests must be regarded as highly satisfactory.

10. *They should be of practical use in musical education.*

In the case mentioned in the above section, the importance of the figures to the teacher lies not so much in their agreement, as in those where divergencies occur. On surveying the estimates in the light of the test scores, it was considered that some of the divergencies could be accounted for by the difficulties of ranking. In certain cases a boy secured a somewhat higher rank for performance than his test score would indicate—this could be explained by the fact that the boy was industrious; this in itself is useful information to the teacher, as it will prevent him from overdriving a boy who is thus shown to be already working to his full capacity. There were also a few who were given noticeably lower ranks for performing than would reasonably be expected from the test assessment, and further investigation was made. One case alone accounted for 25 % of the disagreement in the two rankings. Inquiry showed that (*a*) he had missed some of his class lessons in the violin, and was therefore not aware of certain fundamental principles, (*b*) he was inattentive, and (*c*) he did not practice. In short, he was an unsuitable person for class tuition. On changing to individual lessons there was a speedy and marked improvement.[2] In a second case, the boy had no opportunities to practise at home, and suitable arrangements were made for him. A third had given up lessons at too early an age, owing to circumstances outside his control, and some help was given in starting them again.

Other practical applications of the tests to educational problems are made apparent in later chapters, or have been given elsewhere (169), and will not be repeated here.

---

[1] The assessment of their performing ability was a difficult task, owing to the various instruments involved, for it is not easy to compare either the playing or the difficulties of learning such widely diverse instruments as the clarinet, the violin or the trumpet. On comparing the two results the tendency appeared to be to rank the strings a little too low, compared with the wind instruments. This is probably because there are more difficulties of dexterous manipulation with the strings, and also, because the subject of phrasing is more apt to be neglected in string playing. Some kind of phrasing is forced upon the wind player, as on the singer, by the problem of breath control, because breathing largely fits in with the slur marks. Therefore phrasing gets early and constant attention from the teacher. With string playing, on the other hand, several bows are required to one complete phrase, and the execution of an exactly smooth connection between the bows when there is no phrase ending, or of the break when there is, is a difficult technical matter; this results in the string teacher leaving the matter to a very late stage in the pupil's progress. Finally, the slurs of the notation correspond to the bowing, and not to the full phrasing, which is left to the performer's own taste. Thus superior phrase playing in the wind player may not always be a certain indication that he has a better appreciation of the musical structure than his string contemporary.

[2] However, he always appeared to lack the necessary character to practise sufficiently to reach the standard indicated as possible by his test result.

11. *They should be simple to apply.*

The instructions to the listener were set down fully on the answer papers, and were read out (without comment) in order to make sure that the examinees were not, by some mischance, reading the wrong set. All long or difficult words, or technical terms, have been avoided, although some easy ones were included in the titles in order to give the adult subject a rapid grasp of the problems, but they were omitted when reading to the children. The answers are simple figures or a single letter. Clearly marked, well-separated spaces are provided for them, and each item is announced on the record. The marking is quickly and mechanically performed by a series of cards which correspond to each line on the papers. The tests can be applied equally well to groups or individuals.

The tests may be applied by the piano, but the scores obtained will not be exactly comparable with those given here, which were obtained with gramophone records. However, the ranking of a group should not be largely influenced by the playing of the pianist, because the tests consist, for the most part, of a choice between two items that are to be compared, and not of any absolute valuation of the performance. Although the actual marks obtained by an individual will depend to some extent on the pianist, the score will still, for a reasonably good pianist, be useful for indicating special ability. The musical age may be very approximately calculated if the pianist can, in the light of experience, adjust the norms obtained with the gramophone records used in this investigation to those he secures with his own groups.

The great disadvantage of applying the tests by means of the pianoforte is that, even with an expert pianist who is constantly practising the tests, slight slips occur in the playing. During the early work on these tests any such item was repeated, as it appeared preferable to give a group the slight advantage of hearing the item twice, rather than run the risk of the judgement being given on some aspect of the music other than the one intended. For ordinary school purposes the results from piano-playing are probably accurate enough, but for psychological work, and especially for the standardization of the tests, the gramophone records are much to be preferred, as any record with a slip in the playing could be discarded.[1]

From this general survey it was concluded that the tests were satisfactory, and could be standardized by their application to as large and representative body as could be obtained, and could also be used for the investigation of the other aspects of musical ability and appreciation that were stated as the aims of this work.

---

[1] When the gramophone records were used, it was found advisable to check the speed of the machine by means of a stroboscopic disk. A good portable was found sufficient if the room were not larger than an average class room, but with the aid of an electric gramophone, testings have been carried out with large numbers in a hall.

CHAPTER IX

THE STANDARDIZATION OF THE TEST SCORES

The numbers of examinees of various ages who completed the 'short series' of tests are as follows:

8 years	69	12 years 673	16 years	146
9 years	67	13 years 561	17 years	96
10 years	109	14 years 277	Adults (18 years	718
11 years	479	15 years 178	and over)	
			A total of	3373[1]

About 350 additional persons did not complete the tests and their answers were discarded, and another 1203 took the preliminary tests in one form or another.

The score obtained by any one of these persons would convey little unless it be considered in conjunction with the difficulties presented by the tests to a person of that age. The estimation of the latter is only possible by an expert and experienced examiner, but the information is to some extent conveyed by the norms (the average marks obtained by a fully representative group of a given age). In order to determine these norms it is necessary to secure groups which, after suitable weighting and averaging, will represent a true cross-section of the population.

In the first place, boys and girls should be represented in equal proportions. In the present case, the average marks at each age were, as Gilbert (46) found using other tests, nearly the same for both sexes, so that adjustments were unimportant.

Secondly, a difference in district may affect the results. With the present tests, schools from various districts in London were used as the main source of data, and the norms obtained from them were compared with those from similar schools in the Midlands, the South and East England (there were also some college students from England, Scotland and Wales). In all these cases there was very little variation, and it appeared to be unnecessary to make any allowance for district in computing the values. Not only have the norms been found to be remarkably constant in different schools, but also some German and some Jewish children were compared with the general average because these races are popularly supposed to have high average ability. However, no very large difference could be found, either in the totals or in the marks for the separate tests. It is of interest to note that, using other methods of assessing musical ability, no very large difference was found between Whites, Negroes, Chinese or Indians by the following workers: Peterson & Lanier (118), Gray & Bingham (50), Johnson (70), Garth & Isbell (43), Allen (2) and Porter (120) and between Jewish and non-Jewish people by Sward (150).

Thirdly, the type of school dealt with is usually important in any cognitive tests. From the figures that were given to me concerning the districts in which most of the testing was carried out, it appeared that the majority of the children below 11 years of age were in the State Primary Schools, and so these gave a fairly

---

[1] There is not such an even distribution of numbers among the various ages as it had been hoped to secure because of the disorganization of school arrangements by evacuation and other war-time measures.

representative sample of the child population.[1] About 2 % of the total under 11 years of age were in Preparatory Schools and the junior departments of Secondary Grammar Schools. This group is so small that it could have been neglected without appreciably affecting the results, but the averages were actually weighted to allow for it. At 11 years of age the children from Junior (now Primary) Schools were transferred to Senior (now Secondary Modern), Selective Central, or Secondary Grammar, Schools on the results of a scholastic examination. From the information received it appeared that for the ages 11–13 years inclusive, the proportion of children present in these types of school was in the ratio of 10:3:2. The data were accordingly weighted so that the numbers from these schools used to calculate the norms were in that ratio.[2]

With persons of 14 years and over a familiar difficulty was encountered in that only Selective Central and Secondary Grammar Schools pupils were available; also there was a considerable falling off in the Selective Central School numbers from 14 to 16 years, by which time the majority had left. In the case of the Secondary Grammar Schools, the majority stayed on until 16 years, and a few remained until 18 years. Thus a truly average sample of the population could not be obtained after the age of 14 years.

There was, however, little difference in the average, or range, of the marks in the Secondary Grammar and the Selective Central Schools, and it was thought reasonable to combine them into one group, so obtaining a second set of norms for the schools from which the majority of adults who are musical are likely to be drawn. These were plotted and found to approximate, as did the true norms as far as they could be plotted, to a straight line up to the age of 17 years, after which the norms remained constant. It therefore seemed legitimate to extend the curve for the true norm for the average child up to 17 years, by making use of the equation for that below 13 years, i.e. Norm $= 3 \cdot 1$ age $+ 23$, from which it follows that the child's Musical Age $= \dfrac{\text{Mark} - 23}{3 \cdot 1}$. These curves have been published elsewhere and are not reproduced here (168).

The averages for the Senior (Secondary Modern) Schools were also calculated for comparison; they indicated that there was a considerable inferiority in the musical capacity of the average child, when compared with that of the average from the Secondary Grammar School. At first sight it might be assumed that the norms were being unduly influenced by general intelligence, but the actual correlations with intelligence were found to be only in the neighbourhood of 0·3. The figures obtained with various groups, including some adults, being as follows:

Using the Simplex junior tests	0·30 for a group of 23 girls
With Burt's reasoning tests	0·32 for a group of 43 boys
With the Terman & Merrill tests	0·40 for a group of 24 adults
With the Cattell III*a* tests	0·34 for a group of 24 adults
With the Group 33 tests	0·20 for a group of 454 adults

[1] Taken from the current L.C.C. statistics.

[2] True norm $= (10 \times$ Elementary School norm $+ 3 \times$ Central School norm $+ 2 \times$ Secondary School norm) divided by 15.

Except in the case of the last group the correlations are between the M.Q. and the I.Q.; with the last, however, the correlation is with the raw scores, as these cannot be converted to quotients. A similar figure (0·33) was obtained with a group of 75 boys, aged 16 years, from Secondary Schools, on correlating their music test marks and the marks obtained in a public examination.

Two of the possible explanations of this correlation are:

(a) That music, being largely a mental process, is aided by all-round mental efficiency—although not greatly, as shown by the coefficients.

(b) That musical capacity is completely independent of general intelligence, and that the correlation therefore represents the degree to which the tests are assessing general intelligence instead of musical capacity.

That the former is more probable is shown by the results obtained by Schüssler (130), Koester (72), Hrabar-Passek (66), Miller (99), Pannenborg (115), Haecker & Ziehen (53) and Antrim (3); all of these took teachers' ratings (i.e. musical achievement) and not tests, as the basis of their estimates of musicianship, and they all conclude that the highly musical are above average in intelligence. Smith & Salisbury (140) used sight-singing as the criterion of musical ability, and their work may be classified with that of Farnsworth (38), Fracker & Howard (41), Weaver (160), Drake (36), Beinstock (4), Gray & Bingham (50), Highsmith (62) and Kwalwasser (81), all of whom obtained positive correlations (of a somewhat similar order to that given here) between musical ability, as measured by a variety of tests, and general intelligence.

The conclusion from all these investigations is that capacity to deal with music is somewhat aided by general intelligence, and that some correlation must therefore be expected with any battery of music tests.

In calculating my own coefficients it was noticeable that the agreement was between a very low I.Q. and a low M.Q., and the disagreement was found where a high I.Q. was present with a low M.Q. In other words, a very low intelligence quotient seemed to be a distinct handicap, but a high one was not of necessity a great help. From this it might reasonably be assumed that, provided a certain unspecified level of intelligence be exceeded, intelligence has but a small influence on ability to perform the tests, compared with other, more specifically musical, factors. It is well known that listening of the type here demanded, or critical listening to music in general, is no easy relaxation, but requires sustained and concentrated attention, and it is suggested that those who are subnormal in intelligence lack this power.

CHAPTER X

THE DISTRIBUTION OF GENERAL MUSICAL ABILITY

A survey of the psychological and musical literature shows that considerable diversity of opinion at present exists on the subject of the distribution of musical capacity. The average person appears to hold the view that people may be divided into two distinct classes—the musical and the unmusical. Many teachers of music would support this view to the extent of stating that some persons might be classified as definitely unmusical; e.g. one professor at the Royal College of Music stated that, in his experience, 'it is better for the student to give up music altogether and to turn his energies into a more profitable direction if he finds after the first few attempts that he is unmusical'. On the other hand, some educationists concerned with music have adopted the attitude that most children are musical if properly taught; e.g. Dolmetsch claimed that ordinary children could be quickly taught to play a stringed instrument in time, and with good phrasing.[1]

The references in psychological literature are rather conflicting and uncertain; thus Schüssler (130) estimates 5–10 % of an average group as definitely unmusical, and Leitner (87) reaches the vague conclusion that the line between the musical and the unmusical is by no means sharp. However, Copp (29), Jakobi (68) and Bernfeld (8) apparently maintain that all normal people are musical except through bad education or emotional disturbances, an opinion rather similar to that of Dolmetsch quoted above.[2]

One source of these conflicting opinions is the different interpretations that are placed on the term musical. Thus those who divide people into two sharply defined classes are often identifying the word with executive ability; on the other hand, Copp used the ability to sing middle C as the criterion of the musical or unmusical (this is such a low standard that it would easily explain his conclusions).

As far as I am aware, no previous worker has carried out any quantitative investigation with a sufficiently large number of persons to be able to determine the distribution of musical ability with any measure of accuracy. Some of the curves obtained in my own investigation are given on pp. 68, 69. From the ages of 8 to 13 years they represent an average sample of the population, obtained by suitably weighting children from different schools; those from 14 to 15 years are obtained by combining the Secondary Grammar and the Selective Central Schools, and those from 16 years onwards are representative of Secondary Schools only. The curve for adults was obtained chiefly from undergraduates of Aberdeen, London and Wales, together with Emergency Training College students drawn from a wide area.

As it is seen, the curves are of the 'normal distribution' shape. The persons are widely spread in ability and, within the limit of experimental error, are distributed evenly on each side of the mean. There is no indication of the double hump that

---

[1] See the *Times Educational Supplement*, 10 June 1939, p. 226.

[2] The adoption of any such principle would, if unfounded, throw an unfair burden on the teacher by setting a standard of achievement impossible to realize.

would be expected if there were distinct musical and unmusical classes. It is nevertheless convenient to refer to the musical and the unmusical, and in this monograph the items may be taken to refer to individuals taken respectively from the highest or lowest 20 % of the population represented in the curve.

Neither would the distribution support any contention that all children are musical, for the curves show that there are individuals, who, even at 15 or 16 years, have no more musical ability than the average child of 8 years of age.[1] Their lack of talent cannot entirely be ascribed to absence of education, because a number of those who were unmusical had had excellent opportunities at school and, in many cases, at home too. These persons are unlikely to make any further progress, for the results quoted later show that the achievement of adults is not greatly different from achievement at 16 years of age. These are people who therefore might reasonably be classified as unmusical.

Nor yet does it support the opinions of Bernfeld and Jakobi, for if lack of ability were due to emotional disturbances, the curve might be expected to show a hump (even if small) at the zero end of the scale due to 'disturbed' persons with practically no ability. Any extended psychological inquiry into how far lack of ability might be produced by emotional causes is outside the scope of this work, but some brief inquiries were made, and from them it would appear that although such disturbances sometimes undoubtedly existed, they were relatively unimportant. A dislike for music was found in some of the musical, as well as some of the unmusical, adolescents.[2] In the former, the emotional factor was often a dislike of music due to compulsory lessons or practice; in the latter, it usually arose because the adolescent had been told as a young child that he had no musical aptitude; this not only caused him to dislike music but tended to make him think that it was useless to try to appreciate or understand music. However, the majority of these persons suggested that the effect of any emotional disturbances were relatively insignificant when compared with that of the absence of specifically musical capacities, and although the emotional disturbances might make the examinees perform the tests a little worse than they would otherwise have done, the sequence of cause and effect was more usually lack of ability followed by dislike, rather than vice versa.[3]

The distribution of the marks of 22 boys who, out of a total of 202 from one school, were considered sufficiently deaf to need medical treatment, was also plotted, and is given in Fig. 13. Although their average is slightly lower than that of the general level of the children of that school, and there is also slightly more skew to the lower end of the scale, the difference is very small.

The test marks of the 202 boys were correlated with the negative value of their hearing loss for ordinary speech, i.e. their acuteness of hearing, as measured by an

[1] Such views are probably influenced by singing or enthusiasm for the teaching of instrumental music.

[2] The mere demonstration of disturbances in the unmusical is sometimes incorrectly taken to mean that the two are cause and effect; often this type of investigation is carried out on the unmusical only.

[3] It was, of course, realized that in any investigation of a psychological nature any immediate opinions cannot be taken as certain evidence, for unpleasant emotional experiences are often quickly repressed.

68

DISTRIBUTION CURVES

(Weighted average population)

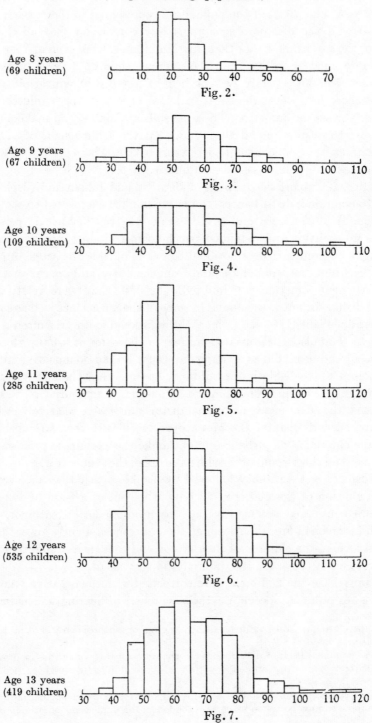

Age 8 years
(69 children)

Fig. 2.

Age 9 years
(67 children)

Fig. 3.

Age 10 years
(109 children)

Fig. 4.

Age 11 years
(285 children)

Fig. 5.

Age 12 years
(535 children)

Fig. 6.

Age 13 years
(419 children)

Fig. 7.

DISTRIBUTION CURVES

(Selective Central and Grammar Schools)

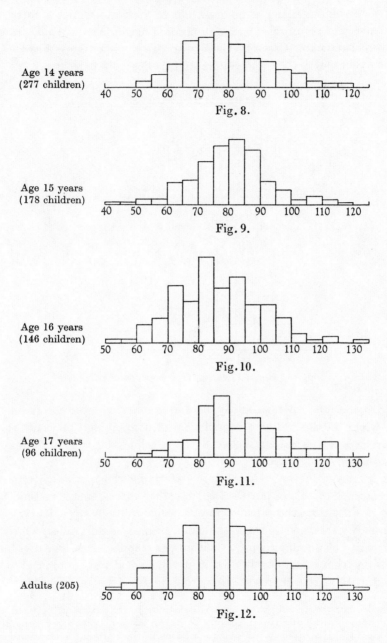

Age 14 years
(277 children)

Fig. 8.

Age 15 years
(178 children)

Fig. 9.

Age 16 years
(146 children)

Fig. 10.

Age 17 years
(96 children)

Fig. 11.

Adults (205)

Fig. 12.

audiometer during the week following the music testing. The coefficient obtained was almost zero, being 0·03 when the average acuteness of both ears was taken, and 0·035 with the acuteness of the better ear.[1] It may be concluded that slight deafness amounting to hardness of hearing up to the loss of 15 decibels, which was the limit of the figures taken, is no great bar to the performance of musical tasks. It is, of course, not maintained that any marked malformation would be anything but a severe handicap. Cases of those who are very actively and successfully engaged in musical activities, and yet are slightly deaf, often occur.

DISTRIBUTION CURVES

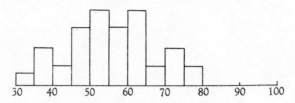

Fig. 13. Partly deaf (22 boys).

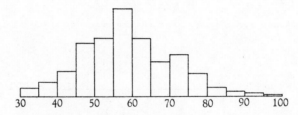

Fig. 14. Normal hearing (180 boys, same school).

The distribution among slightly deaf is almost as wide as among normal children, where in the ordinary school-class of average age 11 years, the lowest 30 % may have a musical age below 8 years, while the top 10 % may rise to musical ages above 17 years.[2]

The distribution curves were used to determine the marks corresponding to various grades. For school purposes some rather more general method of classification is desired than the calculation of musical quotients previously described. It is then only necessary to assess the children into broad grades, which may be used as a guide in assigning them to their proper school classes. The division I have adopted is one that is frequently used in psychological tests, and is as follows:

1. The top 10 % of a representative group is taken as the A grade.

[1] This figure may be taken as indicating that there is little relation between acuteness of hearing and musical ability; it cannot be taken as an exact coefficient since it is extremely doubtful if acuteness of hearing conforms to the normal distribution curve.

[2] The extremely wide nature of the individual differences in a given age group, which have thus been shown to exist, emphasizes the difficult task that the average music teacher has to undertake in the instruction of an ungraded school class. It is to be hoped that, by cross-classification, some grading according to ability for music may, in some measure, be realized in the ordinary schools.

2. The next 20% of a representative group is taken as the B grade.
3. The middle 40% of a representative group is taken as the C grade.
4. The next 20% of a representative group is taken as the D grade.
5. The bottom 10% of a representative group is taken as the E grade.

These are set out in Table III (a) and (b), which are given below. The child's grade is quickly and easily found from either, by comparing his marks with the values there given for his particular age.

Table III. *Score Evaluation in Grades.*

(a) TOTAL TESTS 1, 2, 3

Age last Birthday	A 10%	B 20%	C 40%	D 20%	E 10%
8	over 35	35–29	28–20	19–16	below 16
9	40	40–32	31–23	22–18	18
10	44	44–35	34–26	25–20	20
11	47	47–38	37–29	28–22	22
12	50	50–41	40–31	30–25	25
13	53	53–44	43–34	33–27	27
14	55	55–46	45–36	35–29	29
15	57	57–49	48–38	37–31	31
16	59	59–51	50–41	40–34	34
17 or adults	61	61–53	52–43	42–36	36

(b) TOTAL OF TESTS 1 to 7

Age last Birthday	A 10%	B 20%	C 40%	D 20%	E 10%
8	above 55	48–54	41–(44)–47	below 40	below —
9	63	53–62	44–(48)–52	below 43	—
10	67	57–66	47–(53)–56	below 46	—
11	70	61–69	50–(56)–60	45–49	44
12	73	66–72	54–(60)–65	48–53	47
13	77	70–76	58–(64)–69	51–57	50
14	81	73–80	62–(67)–72	54–61	53
15	85	77–84	66–(70)–76	57–65	56
16	90	80–89	69–(73)–79	59–68	58
17 or adults	95	84–94	72–(76)–83	62–71	61

CHAPTER XI

THE SELECTION OF CHILDREN SUITABLE
FOR INSTRUMENTAL TRAINING

At present most children who take up the study of a musical instrument do so as
the result of their parents' wishes, which are as often based on what happens to be
fashionable in their own particular circle of friends, as on any consideration of the
child's capacities or abilities. This results in a considerable waste of potential
performers amongst those whose parents have not the interest, or financial means,
to give the children the opportunity of having lessons; also, it is an uneconomic use
of the teachers' efforts, which are, in part, expended on some who will gain but little
benefit from the instruction.

This statement may be illustrated by a sample of 271 children, aged 12 years, who
were assessed on their general musical capacity by the present tests. They were
divided on their ability to perform the tests into three broad groups, the AB or
above average, the C or average, and the DE or below average; the percentage
of each of these groups who were studying a musical instrument was then
calculated.

Table IV. *The Percentage of the Ability Groups who are studying an instrument.*

	271 children aged 12 years		
Ability group	AB (Above average)	C (Average)	DE (Below average)
No. of children	103	108	60
Percentage of each group studying an instrument	28 %	28 %	23 %
Percentage of each group not studying an instrument	72 %	72 %	77 %

It may be seen that there was no significant difference in the figures of the three
groups. In the 'above average' (or AB) group, 72 % of the children were not
studying an instrument; this seems a great waste of talent. On questioning them it
appeared that, in many cases, the idea was one which had not previously been
considered, either by themselves or by their parents. The latter are more disposed
to take action in the matter of music lessons and of purchasing instruments if they
have an indication that there is some likelihood of their children's success. By
using the tests this prognosis is possible. The tests will, of course, only indicate
possibilities; they cannot guarantee success where other necessary qualities of
temperament or character are absent (cf. (169) Ch. XIX). By some discussion of

the topic with the children, and a letter to their parents, many were persuaded to commence, and very few were afterwards found to give up playing.[1]

Turning now to the below average, or DE group, the question arises as to the desirability of discouraging those who do badly in the tests from learning an instrument. On the grounds of the general procedure adopted in other branches of psychological guidance, it would appear that an obvious use of the tests is to save such children from a wasteful expenditure of energy by warning them that they would probably find a more profitable field elsewhere. However, a large number of music teachers and educationists strongly oppose this, claiming that nothing should be done to discourage anyone from a pursuit of music. It therefore seemed advisable to obtain concrete evidence on the point, and to find out what actually happened to those of poor ability who took up the study of an instrument.

Investigations were made with a group of 333 boys aged 14–16 years. They were once again divided on the results of testing into three ability groups. The percentages of instrumentalists who had started studying and then lapsed were found for each group, and are as follows:

Table V. *The Percentages of the various Ability Groups who are lapsed instrumentalists.*

333 boys aged 14 to 16 years			
Ability group	AB (Above average)	C (Average)	DE (Below average)
No. of children	84	139	110
Percentage of lapsed instrumentalists	2 %	27 %	40 %
Percentage continuing to play	98 %	73 %	60 %

[1] Besides the letter stating that the child had done well on the test, there were also accompanying details of the prices of lessons and of instruments, and of special arrangements which were made for the latter to be obtained on a hire-purchase basis. Financial difficulties prevented certain children from availing themselves of the opportunities provided. Some of these were helped by the profit made on the sale of instruments to the more prosperous ones; others had instruments loaned. Many of these children purchased their instruments as they got older, or when they left school.

There yet remained others for whom this help was not enough, as they could not afford the lessons. It seems a pity that these children of high general musical ability should thus miss the opportunity of taking up a study that would be a lifelong source of pleasure. Under various authorities there do exist admirable scholarship schemes in music, by which junior children, who have proved their worth as performers, are provided with free lessons at a recognized music college, together with the loan of a suitable instrument. However, these schemes are, in the main, aimed at training future professionals, and they only operate with those who have already gained considerable proficiency in the performance of their instrument. It would appear desirable that the scheme should be extended in a modified form to include those who have no thought of music other than as a leisure occupation, and also to those who have not already begun to learn an instrument but show by such tests as the present series that they probably possess high musical capacity.

The fate of the boys of high musical capacity for whom arrangements for lessons could not

The figures are probably an underestimate of the case, as many boys of the DE group who only occasionally took out their instruments were classified as players. It is probable that such adolescents would take very little interest in their instruments as they grew older, and as the pressure of work and other activities increased.

The table shows that the loss in performers from those of high ability was negligible, but that a large proportion of the below-average children gave up playing by the age of 16 years. It is a wasteful use of the music teachers' time to spend it on the below-average group, in which so many drop their studies, while such a number of the above-average group remain neglected. If the teaching had been transferred from the musically weak to the musically talented, the number of adult instrumentalists could have been considerably increased, with the same expenditure of effort. It would thus appear that it is those of higher ability who are receiving less attention than they merit, rather than the weaker ones.

The above table would clearly show that it is better to discourage those of low musical capacity from commencing the study of an instrument. However, from the point of view of the useful educational work the tests might accomplish it appears important not to offend the music teacher. My procedure with a child of low score who wished to learn an instrument was therefore somewhat modified as follows. The first step was to determine whether the wish sprang from the child himself, or only from his parents. If the former, some attempt was made to trace its source; provided it appeared to be due to some form of musical appeal, it was suggested to the child that he might try for some definite, limited period, and that his progress would then be reviewed. At the same time it was pointed out that the auguries were not very favourable, that he would probably discover that musical performance was not for him, but that there were other fields in which his talents might lie which would better repay the effort he proposed to expend.[1]

As far as the children of average ability were concerned (the C group of those discussed above) their own interest in, and opportunities to learn, an instrument were taken as a sufficient guide.

The discussion in the preceding paragraphs is based on the assumption that the results obtained from a musical test at about 11 years of age will give a reasonably accurate prognosis of the musical capacity at a later stage. The agreement actually obtained between assessments at 11 and 16 years has been very good. The second testing was carried out at 16 years, as this was the latest age at which the subjects could be secured before they left school. The figures are in Table VI.

If the available evidence rested on only one of these groups the results would have been open to criticism on the grounds of the comparative smallness of the

be made was interesting; for investigation showed that at the age of 15 years or so, many would take up banjo, guitar or other dance band instrument. This is largely because such music, being of a simple nature, is easily learnt by such a boy with practically no training, and gives him immediate results. It is a poor use of his talents, but one which does, sometimes, lead to a wider interest in music.

[1] In such a case, the child might find a reasonable outlet for his enthusiasm by a study of such things as musical intruments and their making, or in gramophone or wireless reproduction.

number,[1] but their combined agreement presents a case in favour of the possibility of successful prognosis that cannot lightly be disregarded. The size of the groups that were originally tested was, in all cases, quite considerable, but after a lapse of three or four years they had diminished in size, as individual members had proceeded at differing rates through the school, or had left. Groups that had been planned for 1940 and 1941 were dispersed owing to the evacuation and other war-time circumstances. The figures given are independent, with the exception of those included under Group 6b, which included those boys from Groups 6 and 7 who were tested three times.

Table VI. *The Correlation between Test Results after a passage of years.*

Group	Size	First Testing			Second Testing			Corre-lation
		Age (years)	Date	Tests	Age (years)	Date	Tests	
1	30	11	1935	9 piano	15	1939	7 gramophone	0·77
2	20	12	1935	9 piano	15	1938	13 gramophone	0·77
3	9	12	1935	24 piano	15	1938	13 gramophone	0·93
4	7	12	1935	24 piano	16	1939	7 gramophone	0·95
5	13	14	1937	8 piano	16	1939	7 gramophone	0·89
6a	16	15	1937	15 piano	16	1938	13 gramophone	0·94
6b	9	15	1937	15 piano	16	1938	13 gramophone	0·94
	9	16	1938	13 gramophone	17	1939	7 gramophone	0·98
	9	15	1937	15 gramophone	17	1939	7 gramophone	0·86
7	23	16	1938	13 gramophone	17	1939	7 gramophone	0·93

The correlations for the first two groups are seen to be lower than those for the later ones. For these early assessments the battery consisted of nine rather undeveloped tests applied by means of the piano. In the light of subsequent experience they would not be regarded as a fully representative series. The correlation is, however, sufficiently good to add weight to the total evidence.

The results obtained in the same year from the 24 piano tests are far better; the groups are, unfortunately, much smaller, as so many of these boys had left school by the time that the second testing was made. The first assessment occupied two school periods a week for some months; but it is confidently anticipated that results equally good could now be obtained with the present final series, which takes only an hour to apply, for the correlation of the 24 piano tests and the final series was $0·94 \pm 0·02$.

The agreement must be considered as extremely satisfactory when it is borne in mind that the correlations approach very closely to those obtained when groups are tested twice within a week or so.

When carrying out guidance, the opinion was frequently expressed by teachers that the examinee should in no case be told his score. This seems to me to be a mistaken attitude, for some indication of the child's possibilities or limitations

[1] As the material used for the first testings was so varied the groups cannot legitimately be combined into larger ones.

should be very useful to him. Thus, if he knew that he had a high score, this would in itself be an incentive to take an interest in music, and might well be an encouragement in tiding him over some of the difficult tasks in learning to perform. A low score, on the other hand, might restrain him from the expenditure of energy in a direction likely to lead to disappointment. Finally, the subject's co-operation in the test is more easily gained if he knows that he will later learn the results of his endeavour; this co-operation, as has been previously pointed out, is a vital factor in obtaining reliable results.

CHAPTER XII

THE EFFECTS OF SOME ENVIRONMENTAL INFLUENCES ON INTEREST AND ABILITY IN MUSIC

When admitting the possibilities of a group factor for musical appreciation, Spearman (142) would attribute 'any apparent unitariness presented by musical ability', together with most special abilities, 'to past experience rather than natural aptitude'. According to this the environment should be all important, for the child who lives in a musical environment should have ability, probably in proportion to his intelligence, induced in him. From this, it would follow that musical tests such as the present series would only be assessing the child's opportunities.

My own opinion (which appears to be in line with that which was earlier suggested by Burt (17)) is that musical ability is likely to be, in part at least, innate, although the overt manifestation of the innate potentialities may be greatly influenced by the environment. Any evidence in support of this view must be mainly indirect, for with no environmental encouragement to listen, sing or play, musical talents are not likely to manifest themselves; thus performing ability is always likely to be associated with favourable opportunities, but this does not prove, of course, that the two are cause and effect. It is of interest to note, in this connection, that those engaged in music teaching generally believe musical ability to be largely an innate capacity.

A certain amount of indirect evidence supporting the probability of innate ability has already been mentioned, in other connections, during the course of this work. This evidence is mainly concerned with the small effect that instrumental training appears to have on ability as measured by the tests. These points may be summarized as follows:

(a) Little connection could be found between ability, as measured by the test scores, and instrumental training.

(b) The musical capacity of a child continues to increase steadily after school music lessons have ceased.

(c) The distribution curves are regular in shape. As there is a sharp division between those who learn an instrument and those who do not, if such training affected ability it would be expected that there would be some indication of two humps, one for those receiving lessons and the other for the untrained.

(d) The musical quotient appears to be constant, as judged by testing at 11 years of age and retesting at 16 years of age—in spite of changes in lessons, some having given up, and some commenced, studying an instrument.

However, listening opportunities must also be taken into account. For those mentioned below, the school opportunities, in this respect, were very roughly the same for all the children, and the major difference between one child and another was in the music heard at home. This is likely to affect the child's interest in music, and, possibly, his ability—the latter only if musical capacity is not largely innate.

In an attempt to evaluate the effect of home music on interest, and ability to perform the tests, the children were asked to fill up a questionnaire, which was, at first, fairly detailed. It was found that some of the questions, when used for group application, did not always result in reliable information; e.g. children would state that they listened to radio music for a certain number of hours, but further inquiry elicited the fact that in some cases this listening was real, and in others consisted merely in having the radio programme on as a background to other tasks. The original questionnaire took a considerable time to answer, and so, for group purposes, it was reduced to a simple one on the examinees' interest, the extent of their playing and training, what music they heard at home, the instruments played and who were the players. It was found that children had difficulty in assessing their own interest in music on any finely graded scale, and so they were asked to put themselves into one of four broad classes: A, very interested in music; B, interested; C, indifferent; and D, dislike. They were directed to add plus or minus signs to these classifications if they so desired, but in actual fact so few did that the signs have been ignored in the analysis of the answers.

Of the large number of answers received, those of 333 boys aged 14–18 years were selected for analysis. Adolescents were chosen because they are more capable of giving a reliable assessment of their opinions than are younger children, and as music was for them no longer a school subject, they were more likely to give a candid opinion.

From this group the figures given in Table VII were obtained. It may be seen that approximately two-thirds had some interest in music, about a quarter were indifferent, and a small percentage actively disliked it.

In order to see whether this difference in interest could be linked up in any way with their home musical circumstances, the percentage of each group who had music at home was calculated, and the figures in Table VIII were obtained.

The most obvious explanation of these figures is that a favourable environment is likely to generate an interest in music in the child.[1] This appears to be reasonable when it is remembered that children are very imitative and tend to take up the interests of those in their immediate circle.[2]

Were ability to perform the tests derived from opportunities, the arousing of interest might be the first stage in its evolution; in that case a strong connection

[1] It might be advanced, in criticism of the above figures, that wireless music has been neglected. But it may be taken that it will in general reinforce the home music in so far as, in the home where there are one or more performers, the radio is more likely to be switched on and seriously listened to, than in homes where the interest does not extend as far as anyone playing. Being impersonal, radio music is less likely to initiate interest than actual contact with a musician, and its omission from the above figures is therefore not considered serious.

[2] A discussion of these figures, from the point of view of a comparison of the power of school and home music to generate interest in the child, will be found in my thesis, ((168) p. 412.)

would be expected to exist between ability in the tests and interest. In order to evaluate this into an approximate coefficient, each child's interest and ability had to be expressed in comparable marks. The children had already assessed their own grades in interest, and the median fell in the 'interested' group. In order to convert the grades into marks about this median, whose sum for the whole group would closely approximate to zero, 'very interested' was taken as 2, 'interested' as 0, 'indifferent' as −1, and 'dislike' as −2; the group of 333 boys was also arranged into four sections for ability on the basis of the test scores. In order to get comparable marks, the A and B grades were combined into one AB grade, taken as equivalent to 2; the C grade taken as equivalent to 0; D equivalent to −1; and E as equivalent to −2.

Table VII. *Degree of Musical Interest in schoolboys.*

Interest Group	A (Very interested)	B (Interested)	C (Indifferent)	D (Dislike)
Number	64	162	88	19
Percentage	19 %	48½ %	26½ %	6 %

Table VIII. *Home Music and Interest in schoolboys.*

Interest Group	A (Very interested) 64	B (Interested) 162	C (Indifferent) 88	D (Dislike) 19
Percentage of each group with home music	77 %	47 %	33 %	5 %
Percentage of each group with no home music	23 %	53 %	67 %	95 %

The value of the coefficient obtained on correlating the interest and ability marks was 0·30. The method of awarding marks to each grade must be arbitrary and cannot be expected to give more than a very approximate coefficient, but its smallness seems to indicate that ability is unlikely to have arisen as the result of interest. Questioning showed that interest was more likely to arise from ability, for, as was to be expected, children liked studying a subject in which success came easily, and disliked it if they experienced an uncomfortable feeling of inferiority.

A major object of the questionnaire was to attempt to estimate the importance of the association between the child's ability, as measured by his test score, and his opportunities to hear music at home. In dealing with the problem it seemed preferable in the preliminary survey to omit those cases in which the music was played by the parents, otherwise problems of heredity are involved. The first analysis was therefore concerned with children who heard instrumental music played at home by persons other than the parents. The group of 333 boys was divided into three groups on their ability to perform the test, the above average (AB), the average (C), and the below average (DE), and the percentages of each of the groups who had players, other than the parents, in the household were calculated, and are given in Table IX.

Table IX. *The Percentage of boys of each Ability Group who have Home Instrumental Music—excluding parents.*

Ability group	AB (Above average) 84 boys	C (Average) 139 boys	DE (Below average) 110 boys
Percentage with home instrumental music, excluding playing by the parents	28 %	22 %	27 %

It is seen that there is no great difference in the three percentages, so that it may reasonably be assumed that opportunities, of the limited kind here investigated, to hear music do not greatly affect the child's ability to perform the tests.

If the homes where parents play are to be considered in connection with the effects of environment on the children's performance in the tests, some account must be taken of the effect of heredity on musical capacity. An investigation into the literature on the subject shows that there is very little definite evidence on the matter. The popular assumption is that musical capacity is inherited, and this is largely based on the fact that many of the best performers come from parents who are themselves musicians. This, of course, does not explain the whole position, for there may be highly musical parents whose children are not musical and are therefore forgotten. Scientific studies of family trees, starting from those who were known to be musical, have been carried out by Feis (40), Müller (104), Reser (122), Haecker & Ziehen (53), Mjöen (100) and Mjöen & Koch (101). These studies were carried out by the use of questionnaires, biographies and musical history. This method, too, cannot be regarded as entirely satisfactory, for considerable musical capacity might occur in cases where both parents were unmusical, and so lie unnoticed and undeveloped. Also, the persons considered were designated musical or unmusical, with no graded method of assessing musical ability; finally, the estimates of ability are based on reputation, and so are rather unreliable.

Stanton (145) has followed up six family trees by actually assessing the musical capacity of their members. She used the Seashore tests, and unfortunately did not employ random cases but started from persons who were known to be good musicians. This is apparently the only investigation that has made use of experimental data. She concludes that ability appears to follow Mendelian principles.

The general opinion put forward in the works quoted is that musical ability is inherited. If this be true, it would by itself be sufficient to lead one to expect a close association between musical ability, however judged, and parental performance, for the child of musical parents is then likely to have innate capacity, to grow up in an atmosphere of interest, and also to have opportunities provided for his own development in whatever direction his interests took. In the case of my own assessments of ability, the percentage of the children in each of the three broad ability groups, (divided as before into AB, C and DE on the basis of the tests), who had one or both parents who were instrumentalists, was calculated. The following figures were obtained:

Table X. *The Percentage of Schoolboys in each Ability Group who have parents who play a musical instrument.*

Ability Group	AB (Above average)	C (Average)	DE (Below average)
Number of schoolboys in the group	84	139	110
Percentage of each separate group where:			
(1) Neither parent plays	67 %	78 %	83 %
(2) One parent only plays	25 %	20 %	16 %
(3) Both parents play	8 %	2 %	1 %

It is seen that the relative proportions of non-playing parents to playing parents is 182:18 (approximately 10:1) for the below-average group, and 159:41 (approximately 4:1) for the above-average group. However, playing by the parent is, to some degree, indicative of musical capacity, for it has already been shown that those of low musical capacity tend to give up playing as they get older (page 73). It would appear, therefore, that the figures could be satisfactorily interpreted as being a result of the inheritance of musical capacity. Those who feel that ability to do the tests is dependent on environmental influences might be inclined to interpret the figures by assuming that parental playing is a more powerful environmental factor than is the playing of others in the home. However, some evidence that this is not necessarily the case is given by the following figures:

Table XI. *Percentage of Children of each Interest Group who have Instrumental Music at home.*

Interest grade	A (Very interested)	B (Interested)	C (Indifferent)	D (Dislike)
Percentage of each group where:				
(1) One or both parents play	33 %	26 %	14 %	5 %
(2) Playing is by other persons than the parents	44 %	21 %	19 %	0 %

As far as awakening interest is concerned it would seem that, as an environmental factor, parental playing is very little different from the playing of others.

My own work has been to evolve a satisfactory series of tests, and the problem of the inheritance of musical capacity only enters in so far as it is necessary to make reasonably certain that the child's ability to perform the tests is not unduly influenced by opportunity to hear music. It has been shown that reasonable opportunity to hear music at home, while affecting interest, does not appear to affect the ability to do the tests, provided parental playing be excluded from the calculations; parental playing, although only roughly equivalent to any other playing in the home in the awakening of interest, does seem to be linked with the child's performance in the test, i.e. if one parent plays the child seems to have a greater chance of being in the above-average than the below-average group, while if both parents play his chances are very much higher. Such evidence as is available seems to me to point in the direction that this is more likely to be a result of the inheritance of musical capacity than of any inculcation of musical capacity (as measured by the tests) by the more favourable environment. However, the subject of nature versus nurture is one which is notoriously difficult to investigate, and the whole problem opens up fresh fields of research in musical psychology which are beyond the scope of the present work.

Although, from time to time, small points have been mentioned which were connected with the teaching of music, the main discussion of the applications of the psychological work to education, together with a large part of the introspective and other information collected as a side issue of the development and application of the individual music tests, has had to be omitted for lack of space, and may be found elsewhere. To a large extent such matters must be in the nature of opinions formed as a result of a long investigation, rather than an integral part of the factual and scientific work. The practical aspects are, however, considered to be important, for not only were they the source of many of the problems dealt with, but also the means by which the theories put forward have been, and are being, put to trial.

Furthermore, during the period of the investigation, certain tentative opinions of a highly speculative nature were formed concerning types amongst musicians. Although the psychology of music must be built up on experimental data, yet general opinions based on experience must be the ground from which spring the problems for future research, and for this reason these matters were also included in my thesis, but again, have had to be omitted from a monograph which is concerned with an empirical approach.

A REVISION OF THE *WING MUSICAL APTITUDE TEST*

It is, I think, no exaggeration to say that innumerable psychological tests have been brought out—the *Sixth Year Book of Mental Measurements*, which includes only the better known ones in current use, lists over 1,000. There is at least as much need today for the revision and improvement of existing tests as for the production of new ones. Further, there is also a need for the study of, and for the spreading of information on, the reliability and validity of any given test so that it may be used in the right circumstances and with full consciousness of its limitations. If a test is used for the wrong groups, or if more faith is placed in it than the accuracy of the tool warrants, more harm than good may sometimes result.

There is a tendency for a test, once it has been published to become frozen. This happens for a variety of reasons. The most obvious is that the intial cost of production may take many years to recover. Obviously, too, a revision is likely to entail some years of research.

Particularly in the sphere of music testing, it seems to me, many tests which might have proved very useful have been composed and then left undeveloped. Others again which have been standardized are still in the same form that they were in some 20 years ago instead of having been revised in the light of experience. It is to illustrate the lines on which revision might proceed, as well as to indicate the broad limits of accuracy of such a test and, incidentally, to review some of the more recent work in the sphere of music testing, that this is presented.

Purpose

The *Wing Musical Aptitude Test* was designed to pick out musically bright children at about the age of transfer to the secondary schools in order to give them the opportunity, if they wished to avail themselves of it, of coaching in an orchestral instrument; the test, therefore, attempts to measure both acuity of musical hearing and a sensitivity to performance. That is the primary purpose and the one which will be kept clearly in mind in considering both criticisms and use of the test.

However, it has been suggested by Mr. Papesch, a music teacher in New Zealand, that the tests may also be used for picking out those students who should be capable of studying music for the School Certificate or other examinations. Experience may prove this to be true, but for the present that must remain a side issue. So also must the use of the test as a research instrument in such matters as the relation between aptitude and such things as interest, emotional reaction, enjoyment, or some aspect of personality like neuroticism or extroversion. Even researches which are mainly concerned with choirs and singing are not of such interest in considering my test as those which bear on instrumental playing.

In the preparation of the tests a good deal of selection and revision was, of course, carried out. In the first instance, various tests used by musicians or psychologists were adapted for use with those having little musical knowledge and were tried out between 1935 and 1936. The results were sufficiently promising to warrant a larger investigation using some 36 tests. These were first played on the piano, but later the most effective were recorded. A preliminary account of the results was published in 1939 in *St. Bartholomew's Hospital Journal*, a more detailed account in the *British Journal of Psychology* in 1942, and further research as a *Psychological Monograph* of the same journal in 1946. The gramophone records which had previously been available on loan, were published in 1948.

Results from the application of the tests to children and students were published in the *British Journal of Educational Psychology* in 1954,[1] and in that paper a description was given of the application of the test to the National Youth Orchestra of Great Britain and of how their criticism was sought.   The most thorough-going criticism was, however, that of Bentley in an interesting doctoral thesis presented in 1956 at the University of Southern California,[2] where amongst other things, he compared the results from testing orchestral and non-orchestral students at high school level.   Looked at from the point of view of my own tests, his results produced some very valuable criticisms.

It is obvious that Bentley's long and arduous study would be wasted if it were not followed by a revision.   This work was put in hand immediately and I will take the points in the order mentioned by Bentley and show how far I have been able to meet or answer these criticisms.

Marking

The easiest system of marking is to make use of machines.   An answer paper was designed to make this possible, but as marking machines are not yet available in Great Britain and as their use means sending papers away instead of being able to obtain immediate results, this style was only used in the U.S.A.   However, answer papers of the same type which can be marked by the use of a punched card were printed and are now available.

The Use of Percentile Norms

At present the norms are given in terms of musical age or, alternatively, in terms of five groups only.   The groupings were obtained by dividing the distribution curves for each age into five appropriate sections.   It would be easy enough to divide these curves into sections of 100 instead of 5, but I have hesitated to do this as it gives an appearance of a fine degree of accuracy to the test results which, in fact, does not exist. I feel that it is misleading to express the results of any test in terms which are finer than the original possibilities of marking.   If the results are expressed in five broad grades only, then music teachers and administrators are not so likely to make fine distinctions between candidates which are not really justified by the powers of discrimination of the test.   I am, therefore, disposed to continue with my system of only five grades till further experience demands a change.

The Quality of Recording

It is obviously desirable to have as musical a recording as possible.   It does not, however, appear, from using different recordings, to be very important for testing purposes, provided, of course, that the recording is test-worthy, i.e. it is sufficiently clear for the good candidates to be able to do the tasks set.   The first test, which asks how many notes are in a played chord, is the most critical from the point of view of recording as only the very best machines can produce a chord sufficiently free from slight variations in pitch not to be noticeable to a keen ear.   However, a goodly number of the best candidates actually score full marks on this difficult test, showing that the problem is capable of solution.

The tape has the undoubted advantage that, given the machine, the prime cost of a set of new recordings is merely that of a tape, whereas with discs it means a set of new masters, which is expensive.   Thus, modified tapes, like those for use with the blind, or those in other languages, or with items in a different order, have been made.[3]

[1] Herbert D. Wing, ' Some Applications of Test Results to Education in Music ', *Brit. Jour. Ed. Psych.* XXIV (November 1954), 161–70.

[2] Richard R. Bentley ' A Critical Comparison of Certain Musical Aptitude Tests ', unpublished doctoral dissertation (University of Southern California, 1956).

[3] Herbert D. Wing, *Tests of Musical Intelligence* [tape, manual and literature] (National Foundation for Educational Research, 19, Wimpole Street, London, W.1).

Norms

Bentley suggests that norms should be based on 1,000 per age group which would mean 11,000 in my own case. The numbers of those tested for which I have figures is now within measurable distance of this total, but is still somewhat below that desired for the adolescent age groups—both in actual numbers and in being truly representative.

Fatigue

That the complete test is fatiguing has been admitted from the early days when I suggested that the testing might be carried out in two parts. However, the fact that the test is no easy relaxation was not felt to be any great detriment—on the contrary, it might actually help to select those who had 'staying power' for serious music. Nevertheless, in use, there have been many demands from serious investigators for a shorter test. Bentley himself suggests that 'if only a short testing time is available the sub-total for the Wing tests of 1, 2 and 3 would be the best single measure.' Certainly for those of a musical age of below about ten years, it is largely a waste of time to give the last four rather advanced tests. I have, therefore, prepared norms for the total of these tests but I still recommend that, for the most advanced assessments, this shall be only the first stage of the testing.

Any saving of time in shortening the first three tests would be very small—for they only take 12 minutes playing time for the 3—but a saving of about 15 minutes can be obtained by omitting 6 out of 20 items in the last 4 sub-tests. To find the effect of such a curtailment, six arbitrarily chosen items were removed from a set of test results obtained from 100 students of the National Youth Orchestra and the result correlated with the full test. A correlation of .96 was obtained; this indicates, of course, that the efficiency for that particular group had not been appreciably reduced by shortening. On revision, therefore, the test was shortened by this amount, the items removed being selected by the item analysis described below.

The Influence of Sex

In my early work I did carry out some rather elementary investigations on the difference between the sexes in musical aptitude. Although some differences were found, they were not sufficiently marked to indicate that this factor was of any significance in preparing norms. Further checks indicate that the earlier assumption was justified. This is not, of course, to say that there may not be interesting differences in the rate of development of various aspects of music which would be worth investigation, but that is a matter outside the scope of this book.

The Influence of Intelligence

As success in so much school work is bound up with the level of the child's general intelligence, the relationship between intelligence and musical aptitude assumes some importance; this is because if, as seems to be the case, the correlation is comparatively small, music may provide an avenue of success for those who are not in the top rank of intelligence. This does not mean to say that intelligence is not a help in using musical aptitude—it must always be so—but that the musical side is the primary necessity, i.e. high intelligence cannot induce musical aptitude if there is no musical sensitivity in the child. My aforementioned article of 1954 dealt with this subject at about the same time as Bentley produced his thesis, and Mr. Newton's investigation, mentioned later, on selecting pupils for the study of musical instruments, makes a valuable contribution towards putting general and musical aptitudes in their proper perspective. However, in view of the educational implications, I cannot but agree that the topic still needs further research.

Item Analysis

This has now been carried out by a detailed examination of 100 of the answer papers of the National Youth Orchestra in order to discover how many students gave the right answer, and how many some other answers, for each item of the test. Any item which the students found difficult might be so because the problem set was musically advanced, or because some other irrelevant factors, such as ambiguity, made the question difficult to answer. The results from such a detailed examination would take too long to give—it is sufficient for our present purposes to say that any item which appeared to be in any way doubtful was removed or modified; also that the last four were shortened to 14 items instead of 20.[1]

Correlations and Factor Analysis

The process of item analysis can be extended to consider the efficiency of each sub-test. To do this, the intercorrelations of the sub-tests were calculated. It was found that each of them correlated reasonably well with the total of the tests but not too highly with the others. It is therefore reasonable to assume that each sub-test is contributing its distinctive quota to the total assessment without overlapping too much with any other sub-test.

There is a further stage in comparing tests or sub-tests which may be carried out with these correlations, i.e. a factor analysis. This was used by Franklin[2] in 1956 and in 1959 by Faulds.[3] Factor analysis is really a method of expressing the correlations in terms of a number of factors, each with its own loading. These loadings are then interpreted, according to one's own fancy, either before or after rotation. Of the tests Faulds used, my own showed the highest loading for 'music' (Factor I) in the unrotated factors—if the factors are rotated then the order is, of course, changed. Naturally enough in the circumstances, I prefer to follow the usual British custom of interpreting unrotated factors!

Limits of Accuracy

There were two main points that I raised at the beginning of this chapter. The first was that published tests should be subject to revision from time to time in the light of criticisms which emerge from their use. I have tried to show how the most searching (if friendly) criticism of my own test by Dr. Bentley has been answered by revision.

The second was that tests need thorough investigation to establish their general limits of accuracy. Test compilers, and I am no exception, suffer both from those who would reject tests altogether and equally from those who, like the investigator mentioned above, would take results to four places of decimals, and who forget that there are many other factors besides mental aptitude in the learning situation.

Space forbids my going into my second main point at all fully. I must, therefore, content myself with a mere indication of the results so far obtained. I will take this under the three usual headings: norms, reliability, and validity.

Norms

I have already dealt with this to some extent when discussing the relative merits of the use of percentiles and of five broad grades only. The shortening of the test in the

---

[1] Owing to the kindness of the lecturers concerned, an opportunity was taken during a visit to the Eastman School of Music to test an instrumental group. Such a test is, of course, a test of the Test and not of the students who all did very well. An item analysis of the results showed that there was an element of doubt in only 4 out of the 136 items. A new recording, was prepared in which special attention was given to these particular items.

[2] E. Franklin, *Tonality as a Basis for the Study of Musical Talent* (Goteberg: Cumperts Forlag, 1956).

[3] B. Faulds, 'The Perception of Pitch in Music', unpublished master's thesis (Princeton University, 1959).

revised form must mean that the fine degrees of discriminations are now even less possible, and all I said about regarding the marks as indicating broad grades only is now even more applicable.

The results from testing about 8,000 children, so far, show that the norms for the first three tests are not changed to any marked extent, while the norms for the total test follow a similar pattern to those for the original version, but naturally enough, with reduced totals. Work is still proceeding on checking the norms as it is with reliability and validity.

Reliability

As the tests are designed to select those of high aptitude for the study of instrumental music, it would seem appropriate (and to me essential) to assess the reliability on groups of reasonably high aptitude, and to test the validity against instrumental performance. Any discussion of low aptitude scores and of aspects of music such as singing or examination theory are, as I said before, a side issue.

Reliability is the capacity of the test to give consistent scores. The reliability is most easily calculated by the split-half method of comparing the two halves of one testing. For this purpose the answers to the test of a group of 100 music teachers were divided into the odd and even questions and correlated. The figure came to .9 when corrected for the full test—a highly satisfactory figure for an aesthetic test. (Completed answer papers for the calculation were obtained through the kindness of Mr. Papesch and of the teachers and organizers on the Cambridge, New Zealand, Music Course.) The calculation may also be made by testing the same group twice—but it requires some very self-sacrificing students to undergo quite a gruelling test a second time for the benefit of science. Nevertheless, some volunteers were obtained and the correlation when 19 were tested two years apart was .88—again a good figure. However, groups of non-volunteers gave lower figures (.76) as also did children, as tested by Mr. Cleak of Bristol.[1] The reliability is thus a function of the group tested as well as the test itself, apparently being lower with children and the less able. Too often, I feel, the reliability is taken as a fixed function of the test, but it seems important to bear in mind when evaluating test results that it also depends on the person or group tested. Thus, if only on grounds of reliability, high aptitude scores are satisfactory, but low aptitude scores should be regarded with reservation.

Validity

Mr. Cleak investigated how far the test results agreed with the year's class marks in music and found a substantial agreement. However, such marks are likely to include such abilities as capacity to sing—which is an aptitude my tests were not designed to estimate. A more satisfactory study of validity from my point of view, since it compares the test scores with ability to learn an instrument, is that of Newton.

It is fortunate that a survey of the selection of junior musicians for the Royal Marines School of Music has been recently carried out by the Senior Psychologist's Department of the Admiralty,[2] with a view to reducing the failure rate among those under training. This admirable investigation is one of the best validity studies to be conducted in the sphere of music testing in the last decade or so. I cannot do justice to it but must be content to give a mere indication of the results.

[1] R. Cleak, ' A Study of Musical Aptitudes of Children in a Secondary School ', dip. ed. thesis (Bristol University, 1958).

[2] G. de C. Newton, *Selection of Junior Musicians for Royal Marine School of Music*. An Evaluation of H. D. Wing's Test (Senior Psychologist's Department, British Admiralty, 1959).

In the paper written by Mr. G. de C. Newton he describes how the test was given to 223 junior musicians under training who were then given gradings into average, above average, and below average by their instructors. There was a positive and significant correlation between these gradings and the test results but little correlation with general aptitude or with the small age range of his particular group of adolescents. There was no significant difference in terms of length of time spent learning an instrument in the R.M.S.M. An item analysis showed that in only 9 items out of 136 did the confidence level fall below 95%. All these figures tend to confirm my published results. Mr. Newton goes on to show that if only those candidates had been selected who scored above a certain mark in my tests, the failure rate could have been considerable reduced.

The General Limits of Accuracy of the Test

Mr. Newton gives full supporting figures for his conclusions. It is interesting to look at these figures from the point of view of seeing how far those who did well in the test did well in learning to play an instrument. We find that of those who did well in learning to play an instrument, 1 out of the 27 did badly in the test and 5 others were on the borderline. Of those who proved disappointing on their instruments, there were 2 out 28 well over the borderline on the test and 4 others who were borderline candidates.

I would expect these results to be improved if, as I recommend, allowances for age difference had been made, and if the test instructions had been used exactly as I recommend in the manual. However, I willingly accept the figures as they stand as the kind of result one might reasonably expect from a music testing. They are, it is seen, on a par with those in intelligence testing, i.e. some candidates are clear-cut cases showing definite aptitude and some are borderline. The probability of the former doing well is high, the latter less certain. In the borderline candidate other factors, such as interest or perseverance, have more influence—strong interest may, to some extent, compensate for mediocre ability. On the other hand, if the child has little capacity to do the hard work required for learning an instrument he cannot expect to make good progress.

The test has appeared to miss one child, and to put on the borderline a few others who, in fact, did well. I feel that this does not matter unduly provided the test be used positively, i.e. as an ability detector as the first stage in helping those whose talents might otherwise be neglected. At the negative end the examiner should maintain a cautious noncommital attitude, for even a bad headache or toothache or an emotional upset at home may place the child in a bad way for doing a music test. If he has talent which has not been detected then he should be in no worse position than if the test had never been given. My own response to a child who has not done well in the tests but is keen to learn an instrument is to tell him to try it for a year and see how he gets on. If he does not make satisfactory progress then his interest can be turned to gramophone records, tape recorders, wireless sets, and similar apparatus for he might well get much enjoyment and happiness out of music even if he has little aptitude.

Generally speaking, it is seen that the tests can be a useful tool in helping the music teacher make his judgment of probabilities of success, but they cannot replace the human contact between pupil and teacher, nor can they take into account other factors, such as conflicting interests or the personality of the pupil, which are likely to be known by the teacher.

Mr. Newton in his paper goes on to demonstrate that if the general intellectual aptitude of the pupil is also taken into account, the selection may be improved—a valuable contribution to a problem which needs considerable further research.

In all the above work on validity the teachers' estimates of the aptitude of the child are asked for, and the test is judged by the way its results correspond to the teachers' estimates. Mr. Richardson, of Manchester,[1] however, has rather turned the tables in this procedure by using the test to compare the assessments of specialist teachers and non-specialist teachers. The test results agree well with the specialist teachers' estimates and very little with the non-specialists'. Richardson uses the results as a warning against accepting the judgment of non-specialists. Space does not permit me to go into the interesting educational implications of this finding beyond saying that it is a point of some particular interest to those in teacher training.

[1] J. A. S. Richardson, ' Music in the Junior School ', dip. ed. thesis (Manchester University, 1958).

Test 1. Number of Notes

Test 2. Following a moving part

More than three notes

Test 3. Memory

Music for Tests 4 to 7

Previous to 1957, the music as given in the Ph.D. thesis was used. From 1957 onwards, 14 items were selected as below and used for each test.

Test 4, before 1957	1	2	3	4	5	6	7	8	9	10
1957 onwards	1	2	3	4	5	6	7	8	–	–
	11	12	13	14	15	16	17	18	19	20
	9	–	–	10	11	–	12	13	–	14
Test 5, before 1957	1	2	3	4	5	6	7	8	9	10
1957 onwards	1	2	–	–	3	4	5	6	–	7
	11	12	13	14	15	16	17	18	19	20
	8	9	10	11	12	–	–	13	14	–
Test 6, before 1957	1	2	3	4	5	6	7	8	9	10
1957 onwards	1	–	2	3	4	5	6	7	8	9
	11	12	13	14	15	16	17	18	19	20
	–	–	10	11	–	12	13	–	–	14
Test 7, before 1957	1	2	3	4	5	6	7	8	9	10
1957 onwards	–	1	–	2	3	4	–	–	5	6
	11	12	13	14	15	16	17	18	19	20
	7	8	9	10	11	12	–	13	14	–

BIBLIOGRAPHY

(1) ADLER, M. J. Musical Appreciation: an Experimental Approach to its Measurement. *Arch. Psychol.*, (1929), no. 110.

(2) ALLEN, M. J. A Comparative Study of Negro and White Children on Melodic and Harmonic Sensitivity. *J. Negro. Educ.* XI, (1942), 158.

(3) ANTRIM, D. K. Do the Musically Talented have Higher Intelligence? *Étude*, LXIII, (1945), 127.

(4) BEINSTOCK, S. F. A Predictive Study of Musical Achievement. *J. Genet. Psychol.*, LXI, (1942), 135.

(5) BELAIEW-EXEMPLARSKY, S. Das Musikalische Empfindem im Vorschulalter. *Z. angew. Psychol.*, (1926), no. 27, 177.

(6) BELAIEW-EXEMPLARSKY, S. Die Auffassung melodischer Bewegung. *Arch. ges. Psychol.* XCII, (1934), 370.

(7) BELAIEW-EXEMPLARSKY, S. & JAWORSKY, B. Die Wirkung des Tonkomplexes bei melodischer Gestaltung. *Arch. ges. Psychol.* LVII, (1926), 489.

(8) BERNFELD, S. Zur Psychologie der Unmusikalischen. *Arch. ges. Psychol.* XXXIV, (1915), 235.

(9) BOGGS, L. P. Studies in Absolute Pitch. *Amer. J. Psychol.* XVIII, (1907), 194.

(10) BREHMER, F. Melodieauffassung und melodische Begabung des Kindes. *Z. angew. Psychol. Beihefte* (1925), no. 36.

(11) BRENNAN, F. Musical Capacity and Performance. *Iowa St. Psychol.* IX, (1926).

(12) BRIESSEN, M. VAN, Die Entwicklung der Musikalität in den Reifejahren. *Manno. Pädag. Mag. Beyer, Langensalza* (1929), no. 1243.

(13) BROWN, A. W. The Reliability and Validity of the Seashore Tests. *J. Appl. Psychol.* XII, (1928), 468.

(14) BUGG, E. G. Consonance Judgement. *Psychol. Rev.* Monog. Suppl. XLV, (1933), no. 201.

(15) BULLEY, M. Aesthetic Judgements of Children. *Brit. J. Educ. Psychol.* IV, (1934), 162.

(16) BURT, C. *Mental and Scholastic Tests.* London: P. S. King, 1921.

(17) BURT, C. *Report of Consultative Committee on Psychological Tests of Educable Capacity.* Board of Education. London: H.M. Stationery Office, 1924, 227.

(18) BURT, C. *The Measurement of Mental Capacities.* Edinburgh: Oliver & Boyd, 1927.

(19) BURT, C. The Psychology of Music. Gresham Lectures 1932 (unpublished).

(20) BURT, C. *et. al.* The Psychology of Art. *How the Mind Works.* London: Allen & Unwin, 1933.

(21) BURT, C. The Analysis of Examination Marks. *Ap.* Hartog & Rhodes, *Marks of Examiners.* London: Macmillan & Co., 1936.

(22) BURT, C. Correlations between Persons. *Brit. J. Psychol.* XXVIII, (1937), 59.

(23) BURT, C. Methods of Factor Analysis, with and without successive Approximations. *Brit. J. Educ. Psychol.* VII, (1937), 172.

(24) BURT, C. The Factorial Analysis of Emotional Traits. *Character and Personality*, VIII, (1939), 291.

(25) BURT, C. The Factorial Analysis of Human Ability. *Ap.* Spearman, C., Stephenson, W. *et al.* Symposium. *Brit. J. Psychol.*, (1939), 71.

(26) BURT, C. *The Factors of the Mind.* Univ. of London Press, 1940; cf. also University College, London, Laboratory Notes, Psychological Lab., 1939.

(27) CHADWICK, J. Predicting Success in Sight Singing. *J. Appl. Psychol.* XVII, (1933), 671.

(28) CHEVAIS, M. Tests d'Aptitude Musicale. *Bull. Soc. A. Binet*, XXXIV, (1934), 115.

(29) COPP, E. F. Musical Ability. *J. Hered.* VII, (1916), 297.

(30) DAVIES, M. The General Factor in Correlations between Persons. *Brit. J. Psychol.* XXIX, (1939), 404.

(31) DEWAR, N. A Comparison of Tests of Artistic Appreciation. *Brit. J. Educ. Psychol.* VIII, (1938), 29.

(32) DRAKE, R. M. Four New Tests of Musical Talent. *J. Appl. Psychol.* XVII, (1933), 136.

(33) DRAKE, R. M. The Validity and Reliability of Tests of Musical Talent. *J. Appl. Psychol.* XVII, (1933), 447.

(34) DRAKE, R. M. What is Musical Talent? *J. Musicol.* I, (Sept. 1939).

(35) DRAKE, R. M. Factorial Analysis of Music Tests by the Spearman Tetrad-Difference Technique. *J. Musicol.* I, (1939), no. 1.

(36) DRAKE, R. M. The Relation of Musical Talent to Intelligence and Success at School. *J. Musicol.* II, (May 1940).

(37) DUNLEVY, E. C. Musical Training and Measured Musical Aptitude. *J. Musicol.* IV, (1944), 1.

(38) FARNSWORTH, P. R. A Critical Study of the Seashore-Kwalwasser Test Battery. *Genet. Psychol. Mon.* IX, no. 5, (May 1931), 291.

(39) FARNSWORTH, P. R. Are Musical Capacity Tests more Important than Intelligence Tests in the Prediction of the Several Types of Music Grades? *J. Appl. Psychol.* XIX, (1935), 347.

(40) FEIS, O. *Studien über die Genealogie und Psychologie der Musikers.* J. F. Bergmann: Wiesbaden, 1910.

(41) FRACKER, G. C. & HOWARD, V. M. Correlation between Intelligence and Musical Talent. *Psychol. Mon.* XXXIX, 2, (1928), no. 178, 157.

(42) GARDNER, P. A. D. & PICKFORD, R. W. Relation between Dissonance and Context. *Nature,* CLIV, (1944), 274.

(43) GARTH, T. R. & ISBELL, S. R. The Musical Talent of Indians. *Music Supervisors' J.* XV, (1929), 85.

(44) GERNET, S. K. *Musical Discrimination at Various Ages and Grade Levels* (1939), Philadelphia: Temple Union.

(45) GILBERT, G. M. Aptitude and Training; a Suggested Restandardization of the K.D. Music Test Norms. *J. App. Psych.* XXV, (1941), 326.

(46) GILBERT, G. M. Sex Differences in Musical Aptitude and Training. *J. Gen. Psychol.* XXVI, (1942), 19.

(47) GILDERSLEEVE, G. *Musical Achievement Test.* New York: Bureau of Publications, Teachers' College, Columbia Un., 1933.

(48) GORDON, K. Some Tests on the Memorising of Musical Themes. *J. Exp. Psychol.* II, (1917), 93.

(49) GOUGH, E. The Effects of Practice on Judgements of Absolute Pitch. *Arch. Psychol.* (1922), no. 47.

(50) GRAY, C. T. & BINGHAM, C. W. A Comparison of the Musical Ability of White and Coloured School Children. *Amer. J. Educ. Psychol.* XX, (1929), 501.

(51) GUNDLACH, R. H. An Analysis of Some Musical Factors Determining the Mood Characteristics of Music. *Psychol. Bull.* XXXI, (1934).

(52) GUNDLACH, R. H. Factors Determining the Characterization of Musical Phrases. *Amer. J. Psychol.* XLVII, (1935), 624.

(53) HAECKER, V. & ZIEHEN, T. Uber die Erblichkeit der Musikalischen Begabung. *Z. Psychol.* LXXXVIII, (1921), LXXXIX, (1922), 265, 273.

(54) HEINLEIN, C. P. An Experimental Study of the Seashore Consonance Test. *J. Exp. Psychol.* VIII, (1925), 408.

(55) HEINLEIN, C. P. Critique of the Seashore Consonance Test. *Psychol. Rev.* XXXVI, (1929), 524.

(56) HEINLEIN, C. P. The Affective Characters of the Major and Minor Modes in Music. *J. Comp. Psychol.* VIII, (1928), 101.

(57) HEINLEIN, C. P. A New Method of Studying the Rhythmic Responses of Children. *Ped. Sum. J. Genet. Psychol.* XXXVI, (1929), 205.

(58) HELMHOLTZ, H. L. F. VON. *On the Sensations of Tone,* (trans. A. J. Ellis). London: Longmans Green & Co. 4th edition, 1912.

(59) HEVNER, K. A Study of Tests for the Appreciation of Music. *J. Appl. Psychol.* XV, (1931), 575.

(60) HEVNER, K. Tests for Appreciation of Music. Univ. of Oregon Publications, IV, (1934), no. 6.

(61) HEVNER, K. & LANDSBURY, J. *Oregon Musical Discrimination Tests.* Chicago: C. H. Stoelting Co., 1935.

(62) HIGHSMITH, J. A. Selecting Musical Talent. *J. Appl. Psychol.* XIII, (1929), 486.

(63) HOLLINGSWORTH, L. Musical Sensitivity of Children who test above I.Q. 135 (Stanford Binet). *Amer. J. Educ. Psychol.* XVII, (1926), 95.

(64) HORNBOSTEL, E. VON. Beobachtungen über ein und zweiöhriges Hören. *Psychol. Forschungen*, IV, (1923), 64.

(65) HOTELLING, H. The Analysis of a Complex of Statistical Variables into Principal Components. *Amer. J. Educ. Psychol.* XXIV, (1933), 417, 498.

(66) HRABAR-PASSEK, M. Verhältnis der Musikalität zu der Schulbegabung. *Psychotechnische Zeit.* IV, (1928), 115.

(67) HULL, C. L. *Aptitude Testing.* London: Harrap, 1929.

(68) JAKOBI, H. Muss es Unmusikalische geben? *Z. Psychonal. Pädag.*, (1926, 1927).

(69) JERSILD, A. T. & BIENSTOCK, S. A Study of the Development of Children's Ability to Sing. *Amer. J. Educ. Psychol.* XXV, (1934), 481.

(70) JOHNSON, G. B. Musical Talent and the American Negro. *Music Supervisors' Journal* XV, (1925).

(71) KNUTH, W. E. *Achievement Tests in Music.* Ed. Test Bureau. Minneapolis and Philadelphia, 1936.

(72) KOESTER, H. L. Uber das Verhältnis der intellektuellen Begabung zur musikalischen Begabung. *Z. Päd. Psychol.* XXXI, (1930), 399.

(73) KOFFKA, K. Experimentelle Untersuchungen zur Lehre von Rhythmus. *Z. Psychol.* LII, (1909), 1.

(74) KOHLER, W. Akustische Untersuchungen III. *Z. Psychol.* LXXII, (1915), 1.

(75) KRIES, J. von. Uber das absolute Gehör. *Z. Psychol.* III, (1892), 257.

(76) KRONE, M. T. *Recognition Test, Rhythm Dictation Test, Tonal Dictation Test.* Ohio: Bureau of Educ. Research, Cleveland Public Schools, 1930.

(77) KRUGMAN, H. E. Affective response to Music as a Function of Familiarity. *J. Abnorm. Soc. Psychol.* XXXVIII, (1943), 388.

(78) KÜHN, W. Experimentelle Untersuchungen über das Tonalitätsgefühl. *Beitr. Anat. des Ohrs*, XIII, (1919), 254.

(79) KWALWASSER, J. *Tests of Melodic and Harmonic Sensitivity.* Victor Talking Machine Co., Camden, New Jersey, 1926.

(80) KWALWASSER, J. *Kwalwasser Test of Musical Information and Appreciation.* Iowa City, Bureau of Educ. Research, Extension Division, Univ. of Iowa, 1927.

(81) KWALWASSER, J. Tests and Measurements in Music. Boston: Birchard, 1927.

(82) KWALWASSER, J. & DYKEMA, P. W. *Kwalwasser-Dykema Tests.* New York: Carl Fischer, In., 1930.

(83) KWALWASSER, J. & RUCH, G. M. *Tests of Musical Accomplishment.* Bureau of Educ. Research, Iowa City, Extension Division, Univ. of Iowa, 1927.

(84) LAMP, C. J. & KEYS, N. Can Aptitude for Specific Musical Instruments be Predicted? *Amer. J. Educ. Psychol.* XXVI, (1935), 587.

(85) LARSON, W. S. Prediction of Success in Instrumental Music. *Psychol. Mon.* XL, (1930), no. 181, 33.

(86) LEON, JOBERT. Addenda to the Psychopathology of Everyday Life. *Psychoanal. Rev.* (1931), 154.

(87) LEITNER, H. Uber Musikbegabung. *Intern. Zeit. für Indiv. Psychol.* V, (1927), 379.

(88) LOWERY, H. Cadence and Phrase Tests of Musical Talent. *Brit. J. Psychol.* XVII, (1926), 111.

(89) LOWERY, H. Musical Memory. *Brit. J. Psychol.* XIX, (1929) 397.

(90) LOWERY, H. Estimation of Musical Capacity. *Proc. Manch. Lit. Phil. Soc.* LXXVI, (1932), no. 6.

(91) LOWERY, H. The Integrative Theory of Musical Talent. *J. Musicol.* II, (May 1940).

(92) LUNDIN, R. W. A Preliminary Report on some New Tests of Musical Ability. *J. App. Psychol.* XXVIII, (1944), 393.

(93) MADISON, T. H. Interval Discrimination. *Arch. Psychol.* 1942, no. 268.

(94) MAINWARING, J. Experiments on the Analysis of Cognitive Processes involved in Musical Ability. *Brit. J. Educ. Psychol.* I, (1931), 182.

(95) MAINWARING, J. Kinaesthetic Factors in the Recall of Musical Experience. *Brit. J. Psychol.* XXIII, (1933), 284.

(95a) MAINWARING, J. The Assessment of Musical Ability. *Brit. J. Educ. Psychol.* XVII, (1947), 83.

(96) MALTZEW, C. V. Absolutes Tonbewusstsein und Musikalität. *Psychotech. Z.* III, (1928), 111.

(97) MAVILL, G. & MULL, H.K. A Further Study of Preferred Regions in Musical Compositions and the effect of Repetition. *Amer. J. Psychol.* LV, (1942), 110.

(98) MEYER, M. Is the Memory of Absolute Pitch capable of Development through Training? *Psychol. Rev.* VI, (1899), 514.

(99) MILLER, R. Uber musikalische Begabung und ihre Beziehung zu sonstigen Anlagen. *Z. Psychol.* XCVII, (1925), 191.

(100) MJÖEN, J. A. Zur psychologischen Bestimmung der Musikalität. *Z. angew. Psychol.* XXVII, (1926), 217.

(101) MJÖEN, F. & KOCH, H. Die Erblichkeit der Musikalität. *Z. Psychol.* XCIX, (1926), CXXI, (1931), 16, 104.

(102) MORE, G. Prognostic Testing in Music on the College Level. *J. Educ. Research*, XXVI, (1932), 199.

(103) MULL, H. K. The Acquisition of Absolute Pitch. *Amer. J. Psychol.* XXXVI, (1925), 469.

(104) MÜLLER, G. Die Kantorfamilie Friedrich Richter. *Neue pädagogische Studien*, II, (1930), 182.

(105) MURSELL, J. L. *Principles of Musical Education.* New York: Macmillan, 1927.

(106) MURSELL, J. L. Measuring Musical Ability and Achievement. *J. Educ. Research*, XXV, (1932), 116.

(107) MURSELL, J. L. *The Psychology of Music.* New York: Norton & Co., 1937.

(108) MYERS, C. S. A Study of Rhythm in Primitive People. *Brit. J. Psychol.* I, (1904), 397.

(109) MYERS, C. S. A Case of Synaesthesia. *Brit. J. Psychol.* IV, (1911), 228.

(110) MYERS, C. S. *The Beginnings of Music.* Essays and Studies presented to William Ridgeway. Cambridge: Cambridge Univ. Press, 1913.

(111) MYERS, C. S. Two Cases of Synaesthesia. *Brit. J. Psychol.* VII, (1914), 112.

(112) MYERS, C. S. Individual Differences in listening to Music. *The Effects of Music.* New York, Harcourt Brace & Co., 1927.

(113) MYERS, C. S. & VALENTINE, C. W. A Study in Individual Differences in Attitude towards Tones. *Brit. J. Psychol.* VII, (1914), 68.

(114) OGDEN, R. M. *Hearing.* New York: Harcourt Brace & Co., 1924. London: Jonathan Cape. Pp. xiii, 351.

(115) PANNENBORG, H. & W. Die Psychologie des Musikers. *Z. Psychol.* LXXIII, (1915), 91.

(116) PEAR, T. H. The Classification of Observers as Musical and Unmusical. *Brit. J. Psychol.* IV, (1911), 89.

(117) PEAR, T. H. The Experimental Examination of some Differences between the Major and the Minor Chords. *Brit. J. Psychol.* IV, (1911), 56.

(118) PETERSON, J. & LANIER, L. H. Studies in the Comparative Abilities of Whites and Negroes. *Mental Measurements Monograph*, no. 5, 1929.

(119) PETRAN, L. A. An Experimental Study of Pitch Recognition. *Psychol. Mon.* XLII, (1932), no. 193.

(120) PORTER, R. W. *A Study of the Musical Talent of the Chinese attending Chicago Schools.* Chicago: Univ. of Chicago Press, 1931.

(121) REIMERS, O. Untersuchungen über die Entwicklung des Tonalitätsgefühls im Laufe der Schulzeit. *Z. angew. Psychol.* XXVIII, (1927), 193.

(122) RESER, H. Student Pedigree Studies. No. 44, Inheritance of Musical Abilities. *Eugenic News*, XX, (1935).

(123) RÉVÉSZ, G. Prüfung der Musikalität. *Z. Psychol.* LXXXV, (1920), 163.

(124) RÉVÉSZ, G. *The Psychology of a Musical Prodigy.* New York: Harcourt Brace & Co., 1925.

(125) ROE, A. A Study of the Accuracy of Perception of Visual Musical Stimuli. *Arch. Psychol.* CLVIII, (1933).

(126) RUCKMICH, C. A. The Role of Kinaesthesis in the Perception of Rhythm. *Amer. J. Psychol.* XXIV, (1913), 313.

(127) RUPP, H. Uber die Prüfung musikalischer Fähigkeiten (teil I). *Z. angew. Psychol.* IX, (1915), 1.

(128) SCHOEN, M. Tests of Musical Feeling and Understanding. *J. Compar. Psychol.* V, (1925), 31.

(129) SCHOEN, M. Validity of Tests of Musical Talent. *J. Compar. Psychol.* III, (1923), 101.

(130) SCHÜSSLER, H. Das unmusikalische Kind. *Z. angew. Psychol.* XI, (1916), 136.

(131) SEASHORE, R. H. Studies in Motor Rhythm. *Psychol. Mon.* XXXVI, (1926), no. 167, 142.

(132) SEASHORE, C. E. *The Psychology of Musical Talent.* Newark, N. J.: Silver, Burdett & Co., 1919.

(133) SEASHORE, C. E. *Measures of Musical Talent.* Records by Columbia Gramophone Co. *Manual of Instructions and Interpretations.* Chicago: C. H. Stoelting & Co., 1919.

(134) SEASHORE, C. E. A Scientific Approach to Musical Aesthetics. *Brit. J. Psychol.* XXXII, (1942), 287.

(135) SEASHORE, C. E., Editor. Iowa Studies in Psychology of Music: Vol. 1, *The Vibrato*, 1932; Vol. 2, *Measurement of Musical Talent*, 1935; Vol. 3, *The Vibrato in Voice and Instrument*, 1936; Vol. 4, *Objective Analysis of Musical Performance*, 1936.

(136) SEASHORE, C. E. *The Psychology of Music.* New York: McGraw Hill, 1938.

(137) SEASHORE, C. E. The Revised Seashore Tests. *Music Educators' Journal*, XXVI, (1939).

(138) SEMEONOFF, B. A New Approach to the Testing of Musical Ability. *Brit. J. Psychol.* XXX, (1940); XXXI, (1941), 326, 145.

(139) SEREJEWSKI, M. & MALTZEW, C. Prüfung der Musikalität nach der Testmethode. *Psychotech. Z.* III, (1928), 103.

(140) SMITH, H. B. & SALISBURY, F. S. Prognosis of Sight Singing Ability. *J. Appl. Psychol.* XIII, (1929), 425.

(141) SPEARMAN, C. The Theory of Two Factors. *Psychol. Rev.* XXI, (1914), 101.

(142) SPEARMAN, C. *The Abilities of Man, their Nature and Measurement.* London: Macmillan, 1927.

(143) SPEARMAN, C. *The Nature of Intelligence and the Principles of Cognition.* London: Macmillan & Co., 1923.

(144) SPEARMAN, C. Pearson's Contribution to the Theory of Two Factors. *Brit. J. Psychol.* XIX, (1928), 95.

(145) STANTON, H. M. The Inheritance of Specific Musical Capacities. *Psychol. Mon.* XXXI, (1922), no. 140, 157.

(146) STANTON, H. M. & KOERTH, W. Musical Capacity Measures of Adults repeated after Musical Education. *Univ. Iowa Studies*, (1930), no. 189; (1933), no. 259.

(147) STEPHENSON, W. The Inverted Factor Technique. *Brit. J. Psychol.* XXVI, (1936), 344, cf. also: ref. no. 25.

(148) STUMPF, C. Differenztöne und Konsonanz. *Z. Psychol.* XXXIX, (1905), 269.

(149) STUMPF, C. Konsonanz und Konkordanz. *Z. Psychol.* LVIII, (1911), 321.

(150) SWARD, K. Jewish Musicality in America. *J. App. Psychol.* XVII, (1933), 675.

(151) TAYLOR, E. M. A Study in the Prognosis of Musical Talent, *J. Exp. Educ.* X, (1941), 1.

(152) TORGERSON, T. L. & FAHNESTOCK, E. *Music Tests.* Illinois: Public School Publishing Co., Bloomington, 1926.

(153) TOBIN & ROWLEY. *Tests of Practical Musicianship.* London: Jos. Williams, 1938.

(154) TRABUE, M. R. Scales for Measuring Judgement of Orchestral Music. *Amer. J. Educ. Psychol.* XIV, (1923), 545.

(155) TRAVIS, L. E. & DAVIS, M. G. Relation between Faulty Speech and Lack of Certain Musical Traits. *Psychol. Mon.* XXXVI, (1926), no. 168, 71.

(156) VALENTINE, C. W. The Aesthetic Appreciation of Musical Intervals among School Children and Adults. *Brit. J. Psychol.* VI, (1913), 190; VII, (1914), 108.

(157) VATER, H. Musikalische Produktion. *Arch. ges. Psychol.* XC, (1934).

(158) VERNON, P. E. A Method of Measuring Musical Taste. *J. Appl. Psychol.* XIV, (1930), 355.

(159) VIDOR, M. *Was ist Musikalität?* Munich: C. H. Beck, 1931.

(160) WEAVER, A. T. Experimental Studies in Vocal Expression. *J. Appl. Psychol.* VIII, (1924), 23.

(161) WEDELL, C. M. The Nature of the Absolute Judgement of Pitch. *J. Exp. Psychol.* XVII, (1934), 485.

(162) WIENERT, L. Untersuchungen über das absolute Gehör. *Arch. ges. Psychol.* LXXIII, (1929), 1.

(163) WILLIAMS, N. M., SIEVERS, C. H. & HATTWICK, M. S. *The Measurement of Musical Development.* Univ. of Iowa Studies in Child Welfare, VII, (1933), no. 1.

(164) WILLIAMS, E. D., WINTER, L. & WOOD, J. M. Tests of Literary Appreciation. *Brit. J. Educ. Psychol.* VIII, (1938), 265.

(165) WING, H. D. *Tests of Musical Ability in School Children.* Unpublished Thesis, University of London Library, (1936).

(166) WING, H. D. The Measurement of Musical Appreciation. *St Bartholomew's Hospital Journal*, (May 1939).

(167) WING, H. D. Tests of Musical Ability. *Music in Schools*, (May 1940).
                       (Musikalish begåvning prörning. *Skolmusik*, no. 3, 1943.)

(168) WING, H. D. A Factorial Study of Musical Tests. *Brit. J. Psychol.* XXXI, (1941), 341.

(169) WING, H. D. *Musical Ability and Appreciation.* Unpublished Thesis, University of London Library, 1941.

(170) WOODROW, H. A Qualitative Study of Rhythm. *Arch. Psychol.* (1909), 14.

(171) WRIGHT, T. A. The Correlation between Achievement and Capacity in Music. *J. Educ. Research.*, XVII, (1928), 59.

Recent Publications

BENTLEY, A. *Musical Ability in Children and its Assessment.* London: Harrap & Co. 1966.

GORDON, E. *Musical Aptitude Profile.* Boston: Houghton Mifflin Co. 1965.

LUNDIN, R. *An Objective Psychology of Music.* New York: Ronald Press Co. 1967.

McLEISH, J. & HIGGS, G. *An Inquiry into the Musical Capacities of Educationally Sub-normal Children.* Cambridge, England: Heffer & Sons. 1967.

SHUTER, R. P. G. *An Investigation of Hereditary and Environmental Factors in Musical Ability.* Unpublished Thesis, University of London Library, 1964.

SHUTER, R. P. G. Hereditary and Environmental Factors in Musical Ability. *Eugen. Rev.* LVIII (1966) no. 3, pp. 149–56.

SHUTER, R. P. G. *The Psychology of Musical Ability.* London: Methuen, in press.

WHYBREW, W. *Measurement and Evaluation in Music.* Dubuque, Iowa: W. C. Brown Co. 1962.

DATE DUE
